MOONSHOT SALES

The inspiration that you need to achieve
exponential results in sales

1st. Edition, São Paulo /SP – Brazil

Technical Sheet
Copyright © Augusto Salomon, 2020
All rights reserved.
1st edition – Sep 2023

Text and Edition
Augusto Salomon and Gabriela Gasparin

Translations
Augusto Salomon

Preface
Dr. Adam Rapp

Book Cover
Cleber Machado and Augusto Salomon

Revision
Augusto Salomon

Author´s Photo
Personal file

Based on the Brazilian book
"Moonshot Sales - A inspiração que faltava para
vocês alcançar resultados exponenciais com suas
vendas" by Augusto Salomon and Gabriela Gasparin.
1st Edition – Jun 2019 -Published by Vidaria Livros

Augusto Salomon
São Paulo/SP, Brazil
https://www.moonshotsales.com
book@moonshotsales.com

Contents

To my uncle Valdise (in memoriam), one of the biggest salespeople and entrepreneurs I have ever met.

Preface

The Changing and Evolving Nature of the 'Sales World'

Many people may ask, 'why do we need another sales book.' The answer is quite simple: today, the shape of the sales landscape is dynamic and continuing to shift as new challenges emerge. Salespeople are required to develop new skills and competencies to avoid becoming obsolete. With the availability of vast sources of information, customers have more power than customers of even just a few years ago. This power demands a better understanding of the customer's needs prior to the sales call. It also imposes more demands on their time and more complicated decision-making processes. It is no longer possible to 'sell' to one person. Salespeople are the experts in the sales process, and to be successful they must behave like experts. Sales organizations are introducing increasingly complicated products and solutions, which bring with them higher expectations. These demands require smarter sales, customer goals, and team-selling approaches. Sales professionals must understand how to navigate not only the customer's organization but also the internal sales organization, requiring salespeople to become knowledge managers, knowledge brokers, and information dealers.

The nature of a 'customer' has changed in fundamental ways and is continuing to change as the technologies and structures that support the market increasingly become more sophisticated and more democratic. Just as market transparencies have empowered customers, the tactics, approaches, and tools that enable suppliers to serve customers in a competitive fashion also have continued to change. The new consumer retains an extremely high standard for relevancy in all their interactions with suppliers, who must continually be positioned to answer the question 'How does this (product/service offering, etc.) help me now, and in the future, with these specific aspects of my business? Customers have a reasonable expectation that suppliers will be able to answer this question -- because the quality and level of competition for their business has become higher than it ever has been in the past. The experiences that customers have – the nature of their transactional exchanges and interpersonal interactions – also have become an integral part of the adoption equation.

Customers increasingly expect to have a great deal of attention paid to both their questions and concerns, but also to their needs and wants as well. Because the market has become so competitive, there are always other suppliers out there who will pay attention to an account if that is what is needed. Customers will not be ignored, or they will go elsewhere, taking their business with them. The bar with respect to how much time and energy each customer requires has also been raised. This is why it is essential for customers to understand – and to be helped to understand in very explicit terms and in a systematic way – how you will provide them with value. Translating the attributes of your products and services into a value statement that will resonate with increasingly sophisticated customers requires both a deep and current knowledge of your own offerings, as well as with the nature of your prospective (and current) accounts). Only by acquiring and applying this kind of pervasive, sophisticated bi-lateral knowledge, can value be expressed in an effective way.

Not surprisingly, customers also want to be treated in a unique or personalized fashion that reflects their own set of distinct characteristics and individuality of purpose and focus. It is less relevant to you, tactically, to supply products and services to ten businesses with identical patterns of operation and functionality, than for each of these accounts to feel as if you think about their business as being exceptional. Customers want to feel as if you see them in this way, that you explicitly recognize that they are special, and that you treat them accordingly. Effectively transmitting the sentiment that you view each customer as unique is critical for the maximization of lifetime value.

Finally, the 'new customer' both wants and expects that their current, anticipated future (and unanticipated) problems and needs will be addressed by suppliers in an expedited and comprehensive fashion – requiring a deeper level of preparation and understanding. Any kind of substantial lag between the emergence of a problem and a solution sends a poor service-quality signal for which customers have an extremely low tolerance. Whether contractually bound, or not, suppliers should be positioned to quickly locate detailed and extensive information and technical specifications directly pertinent to customers' interests, and effectively package and transmit this information in a timely way.

The Role of the University in Sales Education and Development

As the nature of sales and the expectations of customers are changing, there is a need for more education and training in the sales area. While many companies do not have the resources or personnel to board and develop their sales force, many aspiring salespeople need to look elsewhere for sales knowledge. One potential area for development is at the university or college level. Research shows that among salespeople hired over a 10-year period, those graduating with a focus in professional selling achieve quota or break-even 30% faster than non-program graduates. Also, these sales graduates' tenure with the company averaged 40% longer. That is an important difference, given the problem most companies have with retaining capable salespeople. Thanks to performance gains and increased longevity, each hire with a sales education netted $175,000 over a hire without a sales education.

The academic environment provides significant advantages in many ways. The academic environment provides significant advantages in many ways. In addition, studying sales in a university setting allows sales topics to become integrated throughout many departments within the business school, along with marketing, accounting, economics, etc., as well as other schools in the university, such as communications or engineering, where many graduates will have to work with and address real customers in their careers on the frontline. For these students, including a degree or focus on sales, coupled with a major or minor, enhances their attractiveness to business recruiters. With team learning, case competitions, and global inclusion becoming a bigger part of the learning process, the academic environment is clearly positioned for this need.

Perhaps the most valuable aspect of sales education at the university level is that educators are not tied to a singular approach or methodology. There is the potential for professors to teach best-in-breed processes. Some training companies may be better at teaching prospecting skills with their demonstrated method or others are better at teaching needs discovery, most sales training only focuses on one part of the sales process. As professors learn about the various methodologies being offered by different training companies, they can put together coursework and a curriculum that incorporates multiple best practices for each stage of the selling process and different types of sales interactions.

Dr. Adam Rapp
Ohio University
Executive Director
Ralph and Luci Schey Sales Centre
Schey Professor of Sales

Acknowledgments

This work would never have come true had it not been for the rich experiences I have had so far - both professionally and personally.

I especially thank my wife, **Letícia**, my children, Pedro and Luisa, my parents, **Valdéa** and **Benedicto**, and my brothers **Ana**, Luís and Lúcio. I have managed to get to where I am thanks to the unrestricted support and structure, they have given me throughout my life.

Also important was the participation of my aunt **Valcide**, an essential person for my success in the sales profession, and an important inspiration for this work.

I must also thank my father-in-law, **José Clélio** (in memoriam), an avid reader and specialist in languages, and my friend **Edson Riera**, an inexhaustible source of sales experience.

Finally, **thanks God** for the opportunity to author this book.

Presentation

Moonshot (or "shooting on the moon") is an English term that has been widely used in the world of technological entrepreneurship. The term alludes to an inspiration that encourages developers to think big when brainstorming and executing ideas for unimaginable breakthroughs. It means an ambitious, innovative, and radical project that seeks long-term (large-scale[1]) exponential results.

I have always been a salesperson and I believe that thinking big, beyond goals, when setting goals is what has helped me most with sales throughout my professional history. So, I decided to title this work you have in the hands of Moonshot Sales. What is the chance we will shoot from here from Earth to the moon and hit it? None, but one must think of the impossible to achieve great achievements.

I started working with sales at the age of 10, at my aunt Valcide's perfumery, in in the small town Itajubá in Brazil, where I was born. There, I spent the holidays, and my biggest fun was selling

---

[1] Abandon the idea of evolving or growing 10% to focus on a solution that results in ten times greater improvement or growth. Source: https://singularityhub.com/2016/11/15/this-is-how-to-invent-radical-solutions-to-huge-problems/#sm.00001txgmsmn16cwcqjxqu1nwy5rz. Accessed February 1, 2019.

perfume to her clientele. Realizing my commitment, I was made official by her as a temporary salesperson. Not only did I return to work at the store over the following vacations, but I decided to innovate: when I returned to my parents' house in Castilho, a city of São Paulo state in Brazil, I appeared with my suitcase full of products bought from my aunt´s perfumery with the money she had paid me for sales. The goal was to resell them to the residents of the condominium. The stock sold out in a few days.

Since then, I have never stopped selling. From my aunt's store, where I was for four consecutive vacations, I went to be a salesperson in my uncle's electronic store, also in Itajubá. At the same time, in my daily life, I was always selling something. I sold old newspapers to the condominium butcher, car wash to residents, antenna installation to my uncle's clients, and even tokens for playing video games in a June party tent. During college of Electrical Engineering, I sold tennis lessons to students and was president of the Academic Directory, which allowed me to continue in business: I promoted numerous parties, shows, excursions, renovations, and improvements involving business relationships.

When I graduated as an engineer in 1997, I even tried to work in the technical field, but it took only two brief experiences to realize that doing technical projects and supervising technical activities was not my dream. I really liked dealing with people. The minor deviation was soon corrected, and within months of my graduation there I was applying for a sales pitch. I started as a pre-sale's analyst at the Portuguese telecommunications company Cabelte. Six years later, I was hired as a salesperson at Algar Telecom, where I have been for 15 years, every moment doing something different, but always in the commercial area. I went through several positions until reaching director. While drafting this book, I was the head of the company's business expansion.

Looking back today, I see that I have accomplished many relevant things in my life as a salesperson. In 2017, I accumulated one billion dollars in sales throughout my career, an extremely relevant and differentiated number, especially considering my area of expertise.

Sales have given me what I always dreamed of, from material goods to the well-being of my family. I have always enjoyed talking and dealing with people, and I am fortunate to do this daily in my profession. In addition to personal achievements, I make a difference in the companies I go through, collaborating to put them on another level, which also deeply realizes me.

Over a lifetime of sales, I have accumulated many experiences, known many stories. This enabled me to come to some conclusions about the profession I chose to call mine. There are many myths and stigmas circulating in the sales area. Common sense says that a good salesperson or a good salesperson is one who has talent, smooth-talking, and is born with a gift for sales. And being communicative is all about becoming a great professional. "I have talent, I can speak well, I'm a salesperson," some think. I am sorry to say that these people are sorely mistaken. It is enough for this "birth communicator" to start working to notice that a friendly conversation makes good friends, but alone does not sell. The more unique the product or service being sold, the more preparation, study and planning is required.

If being talented is not enough to succeed with sales, I bring good news to those who believe they do not sell well for lack of gift. If there is one thing in common among outstanding salespeople, it is far from "good genetics" or "born for sales." What makes the difference is thinking big from the start and combining that personal ambition with much study, training, planning and dedication. It is to have a careful and creative look, to know how to combine a personal dream, a life ambition, with the expected result for the company in which you work. It is to have sensitivity in customer relations, to be considerate, transparent, and helpful. It is possible to be exceptional with sales if you know the customer, have preparation, internal motivation, execution, and resilience. All of this, coupled with enjoyable conversation, is what brings superior results.

The stigmas that surround the profession do not stop there. As much as being a successful salesperson is seen as glamorous by some, some people think working with sales is a fate for those who have failed. That the seller is a villain, a liar wanting to push products at any cost, throats below the customer. These are ideas that need to be demystified. The serious seller is transparent and honest.

In a buy and sell relationship, there are always interests on both sides. Someone wants to sell, and someone wants to buy. Unlike many people think, the good salesperson is not the villain, but the solution. It is important to have this perception, to know that the vision of who offers something is related to the needs of the moment. If a street vendor appears selling water at the headlight and you are not thirsty, you probably will not open the car window to pay attention to it is a street vendor. But what if you are thirsty? It is important for the salesperson to know that he always has the solution to someone's need.

We live in a time of change in the world. In today's exponential era[2], companies are disrupting the way they deliver products and services, innovating and seeking to scale their bottom line. The good seller obviously follows this movement. The merchant profession may be one of the oldest in the world and will continue to exist, especially in complex and personalized sales that require human interaction, eye to eye,

---

[2] It was in which there is a search for results on a large scale with the use of fewer resources and the support of technology.

understanding customer issues and delivering unique and prepared solutions. In the business, we also technically call these sales as consultative because, as its name suggests, the professional acts as a consultant, making a true diagnosis of what the client needs and often offering a unique, exclusive, and special solution to solve the customer´s problem. Faced with an increasingly competitive scenario, with the offer of products and services all the time on the screens of our smartphones, the successful seller is the one who does it differently and stands out for it.

With this work, therefore, I try to help, with my experience, to all the commercial professionals, salespeople and sellers around the world who seek to improve their sales skills, using the moonshot thinking model as inspiration to obtain exponential business results. I try to draw a profile that, throughout my journey, I see to be prominent among those who work with sales: is the exponential seller, who risks getting good contacts, thinks beyond the obvious to reach a goal, is disruptive, innovative, has a foolproof system and creates a virtuous cycle to sell well and always.

This is not about a showoff story, about appearances, but about real facts. I do not bring any manuals or methods to be a good seller, because I do not believe that works. I show through not only my trajectory, but that of colleagues, peers, and various people I have met, attitudes that have resulted in success with sales and that coincide very much with the behavior I see in today's technology entrepreneurs. I am not talking about geniuses, but people who, having a big dream, an ambition, prepare hard, think hard, do not settle for the average, and often risk themselves to excellent levels. Believe me, there is no space for unprepared people who do not dare or risk.

This book is aimed at all the big-dream salespeople, who are looking to go beyond the average, who want to achieve exponential results with their sales month after month, without fear of goals, but treating them as allies, as milestones to be overcome. If you do not accept average results and want to improve your sales skills, and never have to complain about your goals, this book is for you. Get ready to give your moonshot and good sales!

Introduction - The Sales Revolution in the Exponential Era

The sales profession is one of the oldest in the world. Negotiation has always existed, but never can planning and execute have been so necessary as nowadays.

I grew up in a family with many salespeople, the first person was my great-great-grandfather, the "bourdeaux" wine merchant Jean Louis Marie Salomon. A Jew born in the Alsace region of France made a living exporting French wines. He moved to Brazil because of anti-Semitism in Europe. He moved to Itajubá, in Brazil in the south of Minas Gerais state, where part of my family lives to nowadays. I know little about his story, only that he died in the late 19th century and was known to have been a major merchant in the city. When I was young and worked at my aunt's store, many would say, "Augusto is following in his great-great-grandfather's footsteps."

If my great-great-grandfather were alive today, I would be amazed to learn of the changes in business transactions due to the technological revolution. Until the recent past, before the popularization of the internet in the world, from the 1990s, followed by the creation of e-commerce, we were forced to look for a seller when we needed to buy something. Anyone who wanted to buy a television, for example, had to visit a store. The customer only knew the models available upon arrival, and the salesperson was responsible for explaining the characteristics of the product.

Today, it is not new to anyone that in less complex purchases - transactional calls that do not require personalization or trust - you can do everything through the internet: search, compare prices, buy. Even when the customer makes a point of going to the store himself, he is fully prepared with all information about the object or service desired. Often you already know as much about the product as the seller. If the seller interested in making the sale is unprepared, he or she runs the risk of not being sufficiently informed and missing a business opportunity.

Given this scenario, the good sales professional nowadays needs to be trained much more than in the past to remain competitive. This person must have arguments that are not available to everyone if you want to persuade the interested part to buy.

I am not a futurologist to know exactly what the new transformations that technology will bring to the sales segment, but I know that there are already stores, for example, that only work as a showroom for customers to try products and have the experience with what they have seen on Internet. The store does not sell, and the purchase transaction is made online. I believe this model can be applied in several sectors.

The trend is that much of the sales that people make today are increasingly made by machines. Even in the cases of specialized services, this can happen. An example is the tourism market. In the past, travelers went to tourism agencies because they needed information about their destination. You could go directly to the airline and buy tickets, but you would not know the best place to stay and what attractions to visit in the city?

Nowadays, just a short search on the Internet about the desired tourist destination, which soon comes a series of articles and reports, as well as personal blogs and videos with testimonials, opinions and experiences of other travelers, tips on how to get there and what to do anywhere in the world. You can book accommodation from the simplest to the most luxurious on specific platforms. There are also notes and recommendations from other users. Everything is solved in a few clicks.

When we arrive at the destination, we already know everything about the place, we only really must live the experience. We no longer need the salesperson figure behind the agency desk offering packages. Of course, there are still people who prefer this convenience and are still looking for travel agents, but technology has strongly impacted these intermediaries. The salesperson in this business must be clear that he or she sells experiences, not airline tickets or hotel reservations.

The customer today wants to be able to do the entire process on his own through applications. You want to find what you need as quickly as possible without having to talk to anyone. You want to pay and receive what you have chosen on the agreed date. It is the basics. If you look for a professional to help you, you expect something more.

When is the figure of the seller needed?

As much as the sales landscape is changing, the salesperson figure will always exist in society. Maybe not for the sale of wines, as my great-great-grandfather used to do, or televisions, as I have already mentioned, because they tend to need no intermediate. Technology has information about them so clearly and broadly that consumers do not have to talk to anyone before buying online. However, the need for a good salesperson will always exist for complex products and services that require customization.

In such cases, face to face, eye to eye contact is particularly important. These are sales where the customer needs to understand more about what they are buying, seek a specific solution and wants to feel how committed the seller is to effectively solve their problems.

Many business- to-business deals, for example, will always need a good sales professional. Examples of this often happen to me: I have already received sales representatives from technology giants such as Amazon, Facebook, and LinkedIn in my office. All of us have world references in the technology area, but they came to me personally to offer their services in a personalized way. They did it because I am a director of a large company, the target audience for the solutions they offer.

I will tell you about LinkedIn in particular. They came to me to offer a tool that gives potential clients access to this corporate social network. To find me, the commercial manager made use of his own platform. We did not even know each other, and he found through LinkedIn even a common contact between us. At an event where our common friend was, he personally asked him for my WhatsApp contact. Our friend intermediate the contact and I accepted to receive him in my company. I ended up not buying the tool, although I found it especially useful. Interestingly, even LinkedIn, one of today's top social networks, with a super-innovative company format, have salespeople who will personally visit their potential customers. The professional used digital ways to find me but did not give up the traditional face-to-face visit when offering me his product.

Why does it happen? Because when it comes to personalized sales, customers, especially businesses, still need a person who comes in person to explain the benefits of selling, who offers to make customizations, if necessary, who understands the issues and has arguments to show how solve them, which no machine or artificial intelligence does. This happens not only in business-to-business relationships (which we call the B2B sales world), but also in business-to-consumer relationships (called B2C). I say, without fear of making a mistake, that almost all B2B sales are made in person.

As digital as the world is, the presence of a real person to sell will always be necessary in these cases. It is to help with this kind of selling that I author this book. These are sales that require a different salesperson, much more prepared than in the past. A professional who will deal with the individual characteristics and real needs of the customer, their emotions, and their sense of urgency, extracting what the buyer really wants - and sometimes he does not even know right. Believe me, the customer does not always know what they are looking for. The salesperson's job, therefore, is also to provoke him or her to find out what problem a solution or product will solve in his or her life. Sometimes, he does not exactly look for the object of the purchase itself, because so many people have to offer it, but he wants attention and dedication. A good salesperson extracts the essence of what every customer needs. It is a professional that offers interaction, personalization, and establishes a relationship of trust and transparency with the consumer.

The exponential seller

The new context in which we live requires a seller or a salesperson to adapt and prepare, because there will always be a customer on the other side full of expectations, highly informed, demanding and looking for good shopping experiences.

Until the recent past, selling was more passive. Customers bought much more easily. Today, there is an abundant offer of anything we can imagine, and your access is just a click away. The seller must understand that he/she is "selling" much more than just a product or service but an experience. In an extremely competitive world, he must create differentiation for success.

Throughout this book, I will work on the characteristics that represent the profile of this salesperson, who has a moonshot to draw on and follows the revolutions of the so-called exponential age, where innovation is the key word. I describe below some of the features that will be explored throughout this work:

Default Seller

1. (S) He works to hit goals. It is immediate, sells only to make money and sees no benefits beyond that;
2. (S) He sells "standard products";
3. (S) He understands the product very well but cannot go any further. It does not follow trends and cannot adapt the product or service to customer needs;
4. (S) He knows details only about what he or she sells. This seller cannot talk about other issues or contextualize the relationship of your product or service with what happens in the world;
5. (S) He sells the same to all people, regardless of the culture, ethnicity, locality, and origin of buyers;
6. (S) He discusses price and discounts right away;
7. (S) He is extremely objective and cartesian: (S) He sells only the product or service and informs its respective price;
8. (S) He is insensitive to intangibles in the sales relationship and therefore has no convincing arguments;
9. The relationship with customers ends in the sale. The seller sees no advantage in creating an after sales relationship;
10. Credibility is only in the product or service that (S) He sells.

Exponential Seller

1. (S) He has a purpose, an ambition and sells to realize his/her personal dream.
2. (S) He assembles the product or service in the most customized way to ensure the customer's success.
3. (S) He makes adaptations to provide the best benefits to the customer.
4. (S) He is well informed and knows about all the events around the world that affect business directly or indirectly, contextualizing trends in all sales steps.
5. (S) He knows that the sales experience changes according to the client's culture, ethnicity, locality, or origin.
6. (S) He only discusses price after researching and understanding what the customer's needs are.
7. (S) He sells positive experiences, something that satisfies the customer's needs, making it thrive.
8. (S) He considers the human being behind the client during the sales process. Analyzes intangible aspects and seeks to understand what needs will be met behind the purchase;
9. (S) He seeks to have fans instead of customers, developing a relationship of trust and loyalty. He understands that the sale is not the end of the process and worries about the after-sale.
10. (S) He believes that credibility is not given by the product or service being sold, but by the trust relationship established between the customer and seller.

The Four Steps to a Successful Sale

The profile of the exponential seller I just outlined will be explored in detail in each part of this book. I separated them into four:

- Moonshot: Plan beyond the goal
- The discipline of execution
- Closing: from natural flow to "forced decision"
- After sales: the customer is your greatest patrimony.

These four steps are well known in the sales world. Every sale of anything goes through the first three necessarily. The after-sales phase runs behind as a freebie but is equally widespread. What changes in each of them, in the stance of the standard seller and the exponential one, is how to execute them, and this is what I will talk about in this work.

There are several actions and characteristics that drive exponential sales. For this, the salesperson must create an ecosystem that sustains the achievement of the goal always in pursuit of exceeding it. You need to have a dream, a well-defined ambition for selling, and a lot of preparation, study, and planning. You must perform flawlessly and with discipline, value and respect the customer at each visit and identify real needs to be met. With that, closing is almost natural. The icing on the cake is to make a good after sales process not to sell just once but several times.

While the conventional salesperson is only concerned with pushing his or her product or service automatically and moving on to the next customer, the exponential seller makes the sale thinking in provide the best the customer's experience. S (He) creates an efficient system with growth potential far above the standard and does so because he has a higher purpose and believes in herself/himself. S (He) has a moonshot, and that is what I will talk about from now on.

Part 1 - Moonshot: Plan Beyond the Goal

Why plan?

Planning is a keyword in the selling process. Throughout my professional career, I have learned that good salespeople, who are extraordinarily successful, plan well. The chance of success is extremely high when there is planning because you are not "raw" or unprepared to talk to the customer. Remember: All customs sales, those that will not be replaced by a machine, require face-to-face conversation with the buyer. And it is about that kind of selling that I talk about in this book.

Good planning allows you to surprise the customer and increase the chances of closing a deal. This avoids the unwelcome response as much as possible: "Okay, thanks, I'll call you later." Being planned is what paves the way for further negotiations and scheduling a second visit (common in most sales that require customization), which means that the consumer, at the very least, was interested in your offer.

The more complex the sale, the more conversations and visits with the buyer are indicated before signing any contract, because you need to tailor the product or service to the customer's needs and establish a relationship of trust. Being prepared even helps shorten this path by reducing the number of visits before the deal is closed. By anticipating the most information at each meeting, the more accurate you are, and the fewer comings and goings are required. Therefore, the seller or salesperson can never go to an unprepared conversation. If you go, or lose the sale to the competitor, or to yourself.

Those who plan poorly can even sell, only they do not necessarily sell the best product or solution or have the best result for themselves and the company they represent. That is: if you do not plan, it does not mean you will not sell, but you will certainly sell poorly. Planning means getting the most out of a sale, both from the customer's and your point of view. Planning outlines the path to the best outcome a sale can provide for both parties.

The motivation behind selling

One of the points that, in my view, most people make a mistake at the planning stage is not knowing where they want to go with sales. It is no use starting from this stage without knowing what moves them to sell, otherwise they will be selling just for sale, which will not bring satisfactory results. The motivation may be to make a lot of money, but it may not be. There is a stigma that the seller is someone who only thinks about the financial return. However, he is just like anyone else, full of dreams and personal ambitions. The money is only a means to conquer them.

I have always been very motivated by personal and professional fulfillment. I have never sold just to hit goals, but to realize dreams that changed my life. In some moments I dreamed wanted to buy an apartment, in other moments I dreamed of traveling around the world, to be recognized, growing in my career, to surpass myself. In fact, I already agreed to earn less to move up, when I stopped being a salesperson to become a commercial manager - how many of us do not do that? At the time, my fixed salary as a salesperson was not that high, but I earned good commissions, which doubled and even tripled my earnings. When I became a manager, I lost commissions, and my monthly income dropped but I realized my dream (to be a manager).

Today, when I look back, I see how much sales have provided me in financial and recognition terms. The sales allowed me to achieve everything I ever wanted in my life, in these two areas. All the things I have been aiming for materially so far have been able to achieve thanks to sales. I grew in my career within the companies that I worked for, I got many travels, cultural experiences, and many interesting interpersonal relationships.

I strongly believe that I just conquered everything because I always had a truly clear place where I wanted to go. I was always moved by something beyond my goals. This "something" may seem small or obvious at first, but it is essential for exponential salespeople. And I have no doubt that this "something" helps all the salespeople to overcome every step of the selling process.

This excitement for selling is part of my background. When I was 10 years old and started working on my aunt's perfumery in Itajubá on vacation, for example, besides enjoying being there, earning my own money stimulated me a lot. And I was just a kid, I could just play, but I would rather stay in the store and interact with the customers. I began by observing my aunt, imitating her. At one point, she found a way to stimulate me: "You really like to sell and want to help me, let us do the right thing. I will pay you salary and commissions, she said." With this attitude, she empowered me (something important to any sales professional, as I will talk about later). I liked to do it, it was a hobby for me, but at the same time I was already imagining how to buy products and resell in the condominium where I lived when I came back from vacation - a story I told in the previous pages. Even today my aunt is a merchant in Itajubá. It no longer sells perfumes but has clothing stores that are reference in the city.

As a teenager, I continued to spend my holidays in Itajubá working in sales. I started to work with my uncle Valdise. He started from nothing and created an empire of electronic stores in two buildings using his amazing sales ability. With my uncle I learned, among other things, that to sell, it is necessary to be an entrepreneur.

I played tennis for many years, and I was a professional athlete. When I studied at college, students could exchange conventional physical education classes for some sport classes. There were basketball, soccer, and volleyball classes, but not tennis. I had the idea of suggesting a tennis course and got permission for it. To get the word out, I picked up the list of all first and second graders who were required to go to physical education class and I met them personally to offer my tennis classes. I promoted tennis throughout the university. I got 40 tennis students, much more than the other collective sports classes, like basketball and soccer. The motivator of these classes, strangely enough, was to impress Leticia - my then girlfriend and current wife. I wanted to impress her, to show that at 17 I was already able to earn my own money.

After I was the president of the Academic Directory, where I had a strong experience in negotiating, promoting events and improvements for students – it was a wonderful experience, I left the College of Electrical Engineering with a strong negotiation ability, essential for my first job as a salesperson.

I tell these stories to show how much I have, from an early age, a great personal uneasiness, an anxiety to accomplish things. I could never stand still doing the same activity for a long time. Far beyond merely setting goals, the concern for achievement was what always motivated me to sell.

In sales, there is always a goal to be met. It necessarily has a value to be achieved within a time slot. It is usually monthly, but can be quarterly, semi-annually, annually, etc. (I detail this on the following pages). For now, it is important to keep in mind that the goal is always a feasible number. The seller always starts the month (or the period set for goals) with a negative balance and a target to be met. My point is that, before you start planning, knowing what motivates you as a salesperson to achieve this goal, makes all the difference to your success in achieving it.

Throughout my career I have met spectacular salespeople who are equally restless and found myself in them. This restlessness leads to proactivity, to wanting to do things differently. You may not have this very striking feature that is not so explicit about you. But being a little restless is important to any sales professional. The mere fact of having to deal with a goal to be met monthly is unsettling. The sales professional starts every month with a negative balance and needs to live with it. No matter how good you were last month, every first day of the month you must start all over again. It is a pressure that requires getting out of sameness and thinking differently. Not everyone can deal with this constant and unpredictable world.

Usually what makes the seller's income is the commission, not the fixed salary. Often, the seller needs the commission to meet his needs and get what he wants for that period. In my life, I believe I have already hired more than 500 salespeople. I have seen it all: there are people who think that they are salespeople, but when they think about having to make the commission, they are paralyzed and do not move themselves. On the other hand, there are professionals who use this as a stimulus to get organized, as a challenge to be overcome every month, and think: "I want to earn everything I can now. Next month, I see what I do." He or she aims to earn the maximum and achieve their dreams. This is the profile of the professional who does not give up and only does so because he has a clear goal about where he wants to go.

What is behind your moonshot?

The first time I had access to the expression moonshot was in 2017, in a course I took at Singularity University[3]. It was one of the first terms I saw there. As I explained, this English word is widely used in the technology world and means solving immense challenges unimaginably. As meaning itself induces (shooting into the moon), it is to have an ambitious, disruptive, and innovative goal. The goal, therefore, is to achieve exponential results, that is, instead of seeking incremental growth (around 10% per year), aiming at growth above the standard, ten times the current level. In practice, it means thinking big, far away. It is shooting from here from Earth to hit somewhere toward the moon, thinking outside the box, radically beyond the limits, trying to achieve something unbelievable. This is how many companies have produced previously unthinkable solutions. Who thinks small will never be exponential.

Achieving these results requires a change of attitude in the way projects are designed. In the article: This Is How to Invent Radical Solutions to Huge Problems, published on the Singularity Hub page[4], author Alison Berman makes an analogy of the posture of a grasshopper trapped in a glass jar. The grasshopper will hit the cover of the jar a few times to try to get out, until it conditions itself

---

[3] Headquartered at NASA's research center in Silicon Valley (USA), it is an educational institution founded in 2008 by Peter Diamandis and Ray Kurzweil. It is renowned for spreading exponential thinking and the impact of digital transformations in various areas of society.

[4] Learn more at Singularity University website: https://singularityhub.com/2016/11/15/this-is-how-to-invent-radical-solutions-to-huge-problems/#sm.00001txgmsmn16cwcqjxqu1nwy5rz. Accessed February 1, 2019

to fly lower. Moonshot thinking urges us out of our comfort zone to remind us of how capable we are of achieving great achievements. It is an invitation to "open the cover" of our pot of ideas.

An example I met during the course at Singularity University is Impossible Burger[5]. Some time ago, in a dynamic about saving water in the world, Singularity people challenged participants to create a hamburger that consumes less water, given the elevated level of hamburger production worldwide. One of the groups considered making a meat-tasting vegetarian option, so the prototype of the so-called "impossible hamburger" was launched in 2016, which grows exponentially and now even has a branch in Hong Kong. The founders produced the idea of developing a vegetable-based protein that tastes and looks like meat. However, compared to beef, it uses about 75% less water, generates 87% less greenhouse gas emissions and requires 95% less land in its production[6]. While in the course, I went with other students to taste the Impossible Burger. They introduced us to two conventional hamburgers and an Impossible to prove: they are similar.

Usually, the salesperson is concerned in his day to day only with reach goals. But being

---

[5] Learn more at: https://impossiblefoods.com

[6] Source: Época Negócios. Available at https://epocanegocios.globo.com/Empreendedorismo/noticia/2018/08/nenhum-animal-foi-maltratado-na-confeccao-deste-hamburguer.html Accessed April 30, 2019.

exponential is not only reaching goals. It is not selling thinking about earning commission money. It is selling to achieve much more. It is to do this to achieve your dream, your life goals, for you to realize yourself as a professional and an individual. It is innovating as a salesperson and moonshot toward that personal desire. Regardless of your business growing exponentially, you can use this concept to motivate you in your daily work. It is not thinking: this month I sold 100 and the next I want to sell 10% more. But, yes, I have sold 100 now, and next month I want to sell 200 because I have something much bigger to achieve than just that goal. It is structuring your life as a professional so that it happens through sales. It is a change of posture.

Moonshot is not the goal. Because the goal will have to be met anyway. He is the target far away that will help you reach it and, whenever possible, overcome it. It is an incentive to think big. At the beginning of my career as a professional salesperson, for example, I had as a moonshot to buy an apartment. I had my monthly goals, but behind that I dreamed of buying my apartment, and fired at this "moon," which was the property itself, at that moment still distant from me. For the company where I worked for, it did not matter if I could do it or not. For me, however, it was a crucial factor in motivating me daily. For me to buy my apartment, I had to accelerate my sales far beyond the goal set by the company I worked for. The more I sold above the target, the higher my commission was and the closer I was to realizing my dream.

Moonshot is about dreams. I have told you about my career so far, I have always had a personal goal with sales, and that motivated me to be a good salesperson. Being clear about your own dreams and goals is extremely important for anyone who wants to realize yourself with sales. Before you worry about the company that you work for, it is important to know what your personal needs sales will provide you, where you want to go in life, and which of your dreams or ambitions can be realized through sales. I suggest thinking about it every time you start planning. If you do not do this, nothing else will make sense later. Keep in mind the answers to the following questions: What is your personal dream? Where do you want to go with these sales? What guides you about sales?

You will sell better if you believe what you sell

Try to sell only what you believe. It takes conviction and confidence that your product or service is good to sell it convincingly. I have a story that exemplifies well what I mean. I once watched the reality show The Apprentice[7] (Brazilian edition) with host by Roberto Justus, and there were two candidates in the final disputation. He asked both candidates what will be the strength point of your opponent. They both

---

[7] *Business reality show in which candidates apply for a job vacancy*

made the famous good neighbor policy and said good things about their opponents. At the end of the stage, Justus stated that both had just missed the opportunity to get the job. He said that if any of them had said something like "I don't want to sell something that I wouldn't buy," it would have won the program and got the job.

Having a choice, I do not sell anything that I do not believe in. In every company I worked for, I was fortunate to believe what I sold. The products and services were great, and the companies did what they promised. This allowed me to give my word to clients and give them confidence. For example, if I do not smoke or like cigarettes, how can I give my soul to sell cigarettes? I will not be able to do that and will not be a good seller of this product.

But life is not always perfect. There are situations where we need to sell what we do not like, for lack of choice. In that case, we will be able to do this for a slot time, but once we find something better, we will switch options. Therefore, I always say: always try a lot to sell something that you believe, that is compatible with your values, so that you can sell with your heart. Think about the scenario of a new customer who does not know your company, product, or service. If, by interacting with him, you do not show confidence and emotion in what you are selling, he will buy from the competitor who does so. I am not saying that it is not possible to sell what we do not believe in, but it is difficult to be an exponential seller in this situation. You could not link your personal dream or convince people if you sell a product or service that you do not believe in.

Know the purpose behind what you do

I am convinced that all ideas of products or services will not work if they do not the purpose of serving the human beings. Of course, people start businesses to make money, but behind that is the purpose of solving an individual or social problem. Just think of the Impossible Burger example: the product arose from the need to create a hamburger that consumed less water during the production, saving the planet resources and, at the same time, satisfying the consumer's desire to taste a delicious sandwich, whose taste like a regular meat.

Some time ago I attended a lecture in which Uber President Dara Khosrowshahi revealed the idea behind the creation of the company. He wanted to reduce the number of cars circulating in the cities. His intention, by promoting the circulation of cars already available, was to reduce traffic jams and pollution. That was the purpose that gave rise to Uber, he said. Another example is Alexandrino Garcia, founder of the Algar Telecom, the company that
I work for and that celebrated its 65th anniversary in 2019. His desire was to connect the Minas Gerais state country with São Paulo and the rest of Brazil, because at that time the farmers could

not talk with the economic capital of the country. When I was authoring this book, I was already working 15 years in this company, because Algar's values fit mine. It is a company that was born with the purpose of serving the community, that invests in a country and really is different in customer care. If any costumer wants to talk with the company's CEO, he can. I admire that a lot.

Today, a salesperson is more aware of what he sells than he had in the past, when access to information was much lower. To be admitted in a program at Singularity University, for example, I had to write two essays on the following topics: "How would you change humanity through the technology?" And "Imagine you have been studying at Singularity University, and in a few years, a story is published about something truly relevant that you have done. What would the title be? I wrote about my work universe, which is to sell telecommunications services.

The subjects of my essays were how much internet access can help in the region's GDP's growth. When you bring broadband to a city, the place develops both economically and culturally, because people have access to information and that makes people better prepared. I am not the only one saying that, of course.

There are studies from many international agencies linking the growth and development of a region with internet access. A basic example is disease prevention. Access to the internet brings valuable information about vaccines, symptoms, diagnoses, treatments and more. Specifically, in the Brazilian case, makes the population aware of how to prevent the dengue (a common disease in tropical areas) proliferation. This improves the health of people who consequently work and produce more.

I believe that everything we do must be done with the purpose of serving humanity. Considering that this book is about sales, the same rule applies having some purpose behind what you sell is essential; otherwise, there is no prosperity. Having an egocentric goal or just wanting to make money may work for a while but does not sustain the sale relationship in the long term. It is important, when planning your sales, to be clear about your values, purposes, and dreams.

Relate these personal ambitions to what you sell and, in addition, understand the larger purpose behind what you are offering. The more this purpose has connection with your personal values, the better. This is the beginning of planning for you to become an exponential seller.

Know where you want to go

Moonshot necessarily requires a target. To shoot at the moon, you must know its location in the sky. That way, first, you need to know what your true personal goals are behind each sale. Here are some questions you can ask yourself:

Why are you a salesperson?

Why did you choose this way to live among so many possible?

What is your main motivation when you are selling?

Why do you need and want to make money?

What is your goal behind every sale?

What dream or personal ambition will come true with sales?

How distant is the target to be hit?

The goal is your ally

Your moonshot and personal goals are the ones that will bring motivation and inspiration to sell. However, do not forget that regardless of them, in the sales universe there is always a goal to be met.

When we talk about sales goals, as I mentioned, we need to be clear that they are necessarily expressed in a number to be achieved within a certain time slot. It represents how much you need to sell to achieve the required business results. Salespeople often imagine that reaching the goal is their big goal. What I argue here is that behind every goal, it is important to know what drives you to sell. Nevertheless, we must never forget that there always will be periodically a standard goal to be met.

And who gives the standard goal? The goal is set by the company you work for or represent. A recurring complaint from sellers, in general, is that the goal is too high to be met. This is the regular salesperson's mindset. Throughout my career, I have heard this complaint from many salespeople. It is the same as asking anyone if they have a good salary. As a rule, the answer will be no, no matter how high the wage in question is.

It is important to demystify this salesperson's belief about standard goals. When we talk about serious and planned companies, the goal is usually achievable. Of course, there are exceptions. But I am talking about the rules, not exceptions. Standard goals are made within a realistic scenario.

In large and serious companies, the standard goal is usually top-down, proposed by the shareholder or owner. The calculation considers market projections and the organization's growth expectations for a given period. The result value is broken down into sales targets to be met, which are distributed to sales force members. When a goal is sent to a salesperson, it has already been properly calculated. Of course, the shareholder or owner of the company can set an extremely ambitious standard goal. In this case, the salesperson who received it must study new markets or ways to meet the target (I will explain in more detail later about how to do this).

Hypothetically we can think of an example of a large department store specialized in home appliances. Each salesperson must hit a goal, the salesperson goal makes part of the store goal, which consequently is as part of their regional goal, which integrates with the overall company goal. If this company is listed, the target will have been set by the shareholders and, if controlled by an international group, it will come from headquarters in another country. In this example, when a salesperson is set to sell ten TVs per month, that number is part of a whole organization's strategy for achieving the desired profit and growth. This logic is followed by all companies regardless of size. Even at my aunt's store, where I had my first "job," as much as she did not do all this detailed planning, there was a minimal sales number that she needed to make to keep the business working and profitable.

A goal is never high, but rather suited to the company's ambitions within the market in which it operates. However, entrepreneurs need to be careful and responsible in setting their goals. There are mathematical calculations to get to them, which must be done with strategic planning.

Goals need to be challenging but possible. If they are too high, they become unreachable, causing sellers to become discouraged and frustrated. If they are too low, they become comfortable, and the sales potential is not fully stimulated.

Most importantly, you, as a salesperson, know the following: A goal is set to be hit, period. Once its number is given, there is no turning back. Have it as an ally, not as an enemy. It is it who guarantees the longevity of business and, most importantly, who will bring you closer to your moonshot - who knows will not make you reach it or go beyond it? If you meet the goal, it means that the company you work for will thrive, your income will increase, and you will be closer to your dreams and goals. If it will help you accomplish what you crave in your personal life, why see it with bad eyes?

Beyond Goals

In most companies, the more the salespeople exceed the goals, the more they earn. Unsurprisingly, most of the salesperson's income is made through commissions. Therefore, by hitting a goal, the gains increase and, if it is exceeded, they rise even higher. There are no rules which vary between companies, but usually the commission grows after the target is reached, at scales that can exceed ten times the fixed salary (as happened to me, for example). That is why good salespeople look to the goal to go. As high as it sounds, one must keep in mind that the goal was designed and calculated within an achievable scenario. Instead of complaining that the goal is too high, the good salesperson, who is exponential, says to himself, "Not only will I hit that goal, but I will also surpass it. Now how do I plan for this? What strategy should I follow? There is no miracle, and only with this ambition, coupled with good planning, will sales happen constantly and consistently.

Face the numbers: your dream at the tip of the pencil

Once your sales purposes, dreams or ambitions are well defined, it is time to pursue them. The logic is to think: What should I do today, based on my moonshot, so that the result is achieved in the long term? For this, it is important to have a north, and this is done by quantifying goals. This account will guide all your planning.

There is a scheme for this calculation that I have always followed in my planning, whether in the position of salesperson, manager, or director. It can be summarized to answering the following questions:

1. How much does my dream cost?

2. How much do I have to sell to achieve this dream?

3. For whom am I going to sell to?

4. Where is my potential customer?

5. Who is this customer?

6. How to reach the customer?

7. Why does the customer need me?

8. What is the purpose of the first visit?

To improve understanding of this subject, I first focus on briefly explaining each of these items. Later, I will deepen each one of them, exemplifying with real stories that I experienced, step by step:

1. How much does my dream cost?

Go around selling blindly is a big mistake. Before releasing creativity to give your "Moonshot", you need to put your feet on the floor and do some calculations. Every salesperson clearly knows their monthly goals once they receive them from the company. What many do not know is how much they need to sell to realize their personal dreams. The value of the company's goal is nonnegotiable because if you do not meet it, you risk being fired. The exponential seller knows this, and instead of complaining about the goal, he finds ways to incorporate it into his dream, making it an ally.

Since the goal is nonnegotiable (with rare exceptions, as I will discuss later), you must sell at least enough to meet it. Many sellers take this as north and stop there. That is, they are mistaken believing that hitting the company's goal, the personal goal (Moonshot)will be reached as well. When planning my sales, instead of just thinking about the company's goal, I always consider my personal ambition, my Moonshot, and calculate the value I need to make each month to achieve it - I do that up to this day, even being a director. I put down on paper how much it costs to realize my current personal desire, so the closer I get to it, the more stimulation I must produce innovative ideas and sell more. Of course, I do my planning also thinking about meeting the goals of the company I work for, but that is not all that motivates me.

For example, let us say the goal you receive from the company is $ 100,000 per month. Suppose that you reach this goal. The commission to you will earn will be enough to achieve your personal ambition? If so, how soon? If not, calculate how much you need to overcome the company´s goal to achieve your personal dream. The important thing in this step is to calculate a number.

It may be that the value of your commission, hitting the target, is enough to make your dream come true, but it may not. Often you will need to sell beyond the goals to increase your earnings and be able to buy that property you want, make the trip you want, enroll in some course, or simply pay off debts or bills for the month. That way makes it clear how much you must sell to reach that number.

In my case, when I was a salesperson, the company's goals that I received many times did not allow me to realize my dream within the time limit I would like, then when this happened, I planned to sell above the goal to increase my commissions to achieve my Moonshot. There is no secret: If you have a dream and it is big, you must sell enough to achieve it.

2. How much time do I have to achieve my dream??

Once you know how much your dream costs, you should focus on finding ways to earn enough to make it come true. To do this you should also discover:

- How much time do you need to reach the stipulated value;

- What is the average ticket of the service or product that you are selling;

- How many sales will you have to make to reach the goal;

- What is your conversion rate?

Suppose you must sell the fictitious value of $ 100,000 in a month - as I said, every goal has a time slot, and in this example, it is one month. Now calculate: How many sales do you need to make in 30 days to earn $ 100,000? You will soon realize that to make this account you need to know your average ticket. Let us say, in this case, the average ticket is $ 5,000. So, do you agree with me that you will need to make at least 20 sales in the month or otherwise it will not reach $ 100,000?

Conversion rate

Once you have calculated how much you need to sell to meet your goal, it is extremely important to know how many customers, on average, you must approach to make a sale. This is called conversion rate (the portion of customers approached who really will purchase). This is because if you need to make 20 sales, if you talk to exactly 20 customers, you will not reach your goal, as many attempts will not work. We never sell everything we prospect[8]. Let us assume that in your market, the conversion rate is 5 to 1 (one sale for each five approaches). Thus, you will need to prospect one hundred opportunities to make 20 sales and hence hit your goal.

---

[8] Explanation for first-time salespeople: prospecting is finding out who are the customers for your product or service

Once, at Algar Telecom, we provided services for a credit card company - our call center attendants had to sell cards from the operator. We provided them with a mailing to potential customers, and we knew that the conversion rate for these contacts was 2%. This meant that each attendant had to make 100 calls on average to close two sales.

When you know your conversion rate clearly, you can calculate exactly how many customers you prospect to sell the amount you need and meet your goal. This way, your sales planning begins to take shape.

You may be asking, "But how do I know my conversion rate?" If you work for a solid, established company, you will get this information easily from your own manager or marketing area. If you are an independent seller or an entrepreneur or are entering a new market, you will need to discover this number. Look for people in the marketplace who know this background, investigate, look for contacts that work in the marketplace. This is a crucial index to achieving exponential results (I will talk more about conversion rate on the next pages).

3. Who will I sell to?

So far, you already know the total amount you need to sell, how many sales it takes to reach that number, and how many customers you must prospect to reach it, correct? Now you need to find out who will make your offers, that is, identify your target audience, be it consumers (for business to consumer sales) or companies (for business-to-business sales).

This was discovered through market research. So, get to know your area thoroughly, take time to research and analyze it. As I pointed out a few times, preparation, planning, and training are factors that differentiate a successful salesperson from the average. This study comprises:

- Understand what you sell: Know everything about your company, product, or service;

- Know your market: know how your segment and its competitor's work;

- Know your customer: Find out who the people or companies that need what you sell are and can buy it from you.

4. Where is my potential customer?

Once you know who your potential customers are, it is time to find out where they are and how to reach them. In the example used above, it was established that your conversion rate is 5 to 1, so you need to look for 100 business opportunities, then have a list of 100 potential customers to reach and make 20 sales. It is important to know that it is not enough to have a hundred random or outdated names. These 100 possibilities should be active names and with the profile of your target audience - there is no sense trying to sell elevator maintenance services in stairway buildings.

You may already have this list of opportunities ready because you received it from your company. However, if you do not have such a valuable list on hand, you will have to produce it. There are countless ways to find where these potential customers are, from the most basic and classic, such as walking down the street and identifying them in a particular region, or using your network (the all-important networking), to today's most innovative digital tools (like social media and online search tools).

Make use of all these strategies and build your list. It must necessarily contain the name of the right person to speak to, a contact phone number (if mobile or WhatsApp, even better) and, if possible, the address. It is a plus if you know exactly who decides to buy if your client is a company.

It is important to be objective in this step: consider whether there are any geographical or capacity constraints for the product or service that you are trying to sell. Geographic limitation occurs when the prospect is outside your area of expertise. For example, suppose you have identified a business opportunity that is 500 miles from your location. If the customer accepts an offer from you, will you be able to sell the product/service? If there are geographical limitations, there is no point wasting time making the offer. I reveal what happened with me when I sold telecommunications services representing Algar Telecom in Campinas city, Brazil. I once did all the steps mentioned earlier in this book and selected ten potential power utilities companies to buy my product. Then, upon further examination, I noticed that out of those ten, I could only offer the service just for two companies, because the others were in areas not served by my company's network. This is an example of geographical limitation.

The same goes for capacity limitation: If you sell natural sandwiches and a large business group wants to buy daily delivery for its 5,000 employees, can you produce that amount? Consider this when setting up your prospect list and include only potential customers. In another example, consider selling school uniforms and listing among your potential customers students at a school near your business. If you find a way to offer uniforms to all students and all students buy them, will you be able to deliver for all on time?

Many years ago, I considered that one of the largest national banks would be a potential customer, but I thought if I made the offer and the bank wanted to buy internet service from my company for all its branches, I would not be able to serve it. With that, I held back the anxiety and did not make the approach. You must be aware of these limitations before selling to avoid future headaches that can affect your reputation as a seller.

5. Who is this customer?

As you begin the fifth step of your planning, you will already have a list of potential customers, which could become real selling opportunities. In the example used in the previous steps, this list has one hundred names. From now on, before contacting each of these customers, your job is to get to know them better, research them, and try to anticipate their characteristics, quirks, and supposed needs. It is important to know how to present yourself, who to talk to exactly, and anticipate information that might be helpful to that person or company about what will be offered.

6. How to reach the customer?

After identifying your potential customer, the next step is to schedule a visit to introduce your product or service. This approach should be as personalized as possible, preferably over the phone and directly with whoever can decide to purchase. Never make this first contact via email or via social media, let alone the standard ones.

The risk of these texts being deleted even before they are read is quite high. Make calls (or contacts via WhatsApp) and try to make an appointment.

In the example we are using, the job is to contact the one hundred names in the list. If the month has 20 business days, you will need to address at least five opportunities a day. The big mission in scheduling visits is to group them by nearby locations - that is, to organize to go to customers who are close to each other on the same day (in large cities, for example, this coordination makes all the difference for the best use of time).

It is important to go in person to talk to each client. Since the beginning of this work, I point out that there is a type of sale that will always need sellers, one that is personalized, customized, consultative. In this case, face-to-face contact is important to establish a relationship of trust with the buyer. It is during the visit that the seller understands the customer's need and how your product or service will be useful to them. As already mentioned in the introduction to this book, even high-tech companies have sales representatives who take to the streets to visit customers and introduce their products (I have received face-to-face visits from giants such as Amazon, Facebook, and LinkedIn).

With technological developments, these face-to-face visits migrate to a virtual model, such as video conferencing, but by 2019 this was not yet the predominance. However, even by videoconferencing, conversation and human contact will be there. Nothing will be done with just one click through an app, as it does with the transitional products or services that do not require customization (in these cases, yes, virtualization has proven to be a great sales trend - a way to go – and a no turning back way).

Remember this at this stage of planning, and if you intend to be an exponential seller, do not try to shorten paths. In the limit, when it is not possible to make an in-person conversation, the phone or video conferencing applications are alternatives. However, the daily life of the seller is many visits. There is a basic rule: If you do not visit, you do not sell.

7. Why does the customer need me?

It is a mistake to think that, after the scheduled visit, you only arrive at the appointed time with a smile on your face and an enjoyable conversation. The successful salesperson knows that before coming to a meeting, he needs to prepare even more. It is time to do a more thorough investigation than the previous steps. Analyze the prospect and get enough information for a compelling approach on the day of the visit. Deepen as much as you can to increase your repertoire at the time of conversation. Study each case well, try to find out what main client´s problem and try to anticipate how you can best help them. Try to have arguments for the following questions: Why did this person agree to receive you? Why does he or she need your service or product? What might be interesting to present at this first meeting?

If the potential customer is an individual, try to find out the specific universe in which he lives, considering their age, income and identified needs. If this customer is a business, scan its website and social networks, research the industry, its origin and history, if has business units and branches in other locations, etc.

Once you have identified exactly who you will be meeting with, try to find out the personal details of the person. Everything you can find out beforehand is welcome. As much as the buyer is a company, the sales always happen from one human being to another. Know, therefore, with whom you will negotiate. If possible, go to their profile on social networks and find out what they like, what their hobbies and preferences are. Everything is material to get the visit as prepared as possible and make a good live impression.

8. What is the purpose of the first visit?

Each visit has an initial goal. This can be to make an institutional presentation and show your portfolio, show estimates of prices and forms of payment, contract details or answer questions. Of course, the purpose of all visits is to sell, but until then there is a whole way to go. Even though good planning increases the chances of success, selling personalized products or services is unlikely to close the business at the first meeting. The higher the order, the value of the purchase or the level of customization, the longer it will take to reach an agreement. This entire process can take months, with many returns and new meetings. It is therefore important to know your goal in what may be the first of many conversations.

Remember there is no meeting with clients to have a conversation or drink a coffee. This "excuse" is common in the sales world. As much as it really is a relationship coffee, know that the initial goal is to get closer to the customer to make a sale in the future. Be prepared to talk and know the customer better and do not waste your time: stay on and have strategies in every meeting once the salesperson's goal is always to sell.

My learnings when planning sales

After a summary of the key points that compound the first stage of the sales process, I invite you to immerse yourself in the stories, cases, and examples of action that I faced in my career when I made my own plans.

As I hope it has become clear so far, studies, research and the constant search for knowledge drive this indispensable step in sales called planning.

I divide this seller's preparation in two steps:

- One of them I call personal and professional development, which takes place through academic studies, specializations, extracurricular courses, training and knowledge in sales or other areas, language learning, improvement of emotional and communication skills, etc.

- The other I call the market study, which is the technical preparation focused on the business segment of the company that the seller represents, plunging into its universe (products and services), sector, competition, and target audience.

Personal and Professional Development

I believe the most important asset in a good salesperson is his knowledge and cultural background. This is acquired throughout the career with experience but should also be proactively stimulated by the salesperson. The more up-to-date and informed you are, the more repertoire you will have to talk to various customer profiles, increasing your chances of selling. The exponential seller knows this and is not limited to studying only his market or portfolio but is aware of what happens in his surroundings and in the world, opening himself to new learning and experiences.

Knowledge is never too much, and it expands our horizons. I say this without fear because today, when I look back, I see how much the continued pursuit of knowledge has helped me to achieve better results. I understand how much I evolved as a professional thanks to my profile of leaving the comfort zone in search of better results. I only reached a level that I am proud of today because I have always dedicated myself to my personal development. I never stopped studying: after graduating in Electrical Engineering, I did my first MBA in Brazil, but I always wanted to study in the United States and realized this dream in 2013, when I was approved for an MBA at Ohio University. In the course, the approach was general, with disciplines such as economics, accounting, and management, among others. One of the labs I did was finance, and the professor was a stock market investor. He taught how the stock market works. We even invested in a $ 1 million portfolio that the university made available for students to learn Logically, this portfolio had some limitations so that students would not do anything stupid).

This learning has given me a wide repertoire when I came back to Brazil, so much so that I feel comfortable talking with executives, managers, directors, and CEOs of large companies about investment issues, once these professionals are constantly thinking about how to grow and grow, valuating the shares of their companies. Having learned about the mechanism of the stock market and how and why to buy and sell shares served as a valuable tool and provided me greater security in the interactions with potential customers of financial area, allowing me to address how much my services could help them to be more efficient and effective in their business. All this experience also helped me in the approach with big banks. I was able to identify the real needs of financial institutions and offer specific services and products that met them uniquely. I started to speak the same language of these professionals, so I had great successes and I made exceptional sales to the biggest banks in Brazil. That is, an academic experience gave me knowledge that resulted in more sales for me.

In 2017, I studied at Singularity University, as I reported on previous pages. There, in Silicon Valley, my quest was to exercise new thinking and expand my vision of doing business. I searched the place with the expectation of doing something different than I had ever done in my life. I read news about the exponential results of the big tech companies, and I researched where I could develop this exponential mindset, and all the results pointed to Singularity University. I was looking for stimuli to think outside the box, differently to what I had thought up until that moment, to improve myself and make what I do even more improved.

In all these opportunities, I improved my performance in sales, not only because of the formal lessons at the college, but for immeasurable factors such as expanding my network and enriching my repertoire to negotiate with clients. Of course, I do not only observe this in myself, but in peers who have the same behavior and in salespeople who have worked in my team. Those who challenge themselves, are disciplined and never get tired of learning, always have the best performances.

The relevance of cultural background

One kind of knowledge I learned to value early as a seller is what I call cultural baggage. My first job in the commercial area was, curiously, abroad, in Portugal. Less than a year after I graduated as an engineer, I learned that a Portuguese company called Cabelte planned to manufacture fiber optic telecommunications cables in Brazil in my hometown. I was working in the technical area in another company, but I wanted to be a salesperson and I applied for the job in Cabelte Company. I was happy when I was hired as a pre-sales analyst on the condition of to move to Portugal to work while the company was building its plant in Brazil. It was great, when I was 21 to 22 years old, I had my first international experience.

This opportunity was so remarkable to me that I remember the date of departure to Portugal: April 24, 1998. I got there knowing nothing and learned everything from scratch. I had never left Brazil or traveled by plane. While the plant in Brazil was not yet ready, my role in Portuguese territory was to develop proposals for the commercial manager who was in Brazil looking for business opportunities. He sent me the possibilities, and my job was to calculate the price and give him technical support about the proposal - at the time, we made the products in Portugal and exported to Brazil.

I had no idea how to make these proposals. I still have the name of the engineer who trained me, Marcela Teixeira. She taught me everything from technical issues, such as pricing and arguing a business proposal, to interacting with clients from diverse cultures, teaching me about export negotiations.

In the six months I lived in Portugal, I dealt with different people and cultures. I traveled to many countries in Europe, both for work and tourism. Once time, accompanied by Marcela, I had a meeting with Russian customers. I also participated in negotiations with Spanish guy and traveled alone to Switzerland on business to sell optical cables. I learned that it is not the same to sell to people of other nationalities. Each culture acts in a way, and the salesperson must adapt to the customer's customs if he is to have success.

This experience was important to me at the time, because when I returned to Brazil, the telecommunications companies had been privatized and, again, I had to relate to audiences of different nationalities. Who bought the biggest carrier in Brazil, for example, was Telefónica, from Spain. And who bought the mobile telecom operator in Rio de Janeiro was a Portuguese company, Portugal Telecom.

I know it is an exception to have my first job abroad, and I am grateful to have this experience when I was young, but any salesperson deals with clients of different beliefs, traditions, customs, and backgrounds in his daily life, simply because he works directly with people all the time. That is why it is important to know your customers' culture well, if you want to achieve good sales results.

At the end of 2008, I had an interesting experience in this regard. I had been working for some years as Regional Manager at Algar Telecom in Campinas, in countryside of São Paulo state in Brazil, when I was invited by the company to assume the same position in the Rio de Janeiro Regional office. I accepted the challenge, with the idea of applying in Rio the same formula that already worked in Campinas, but it did not work out. In the first months, I had a lot of difficulties, I maintained the performance of my predecessor, but could not meet the goal I received from the company. This happened because I did not understand how the Rio de Janeiro market worked. I had to adjust considering regional differences to be able to reverse the situation. If I wanted to make good returns, I would have to know how the local society worked, and I soon went after closer relationships to increase my sales performance in Rio.

It was a lot of research work that involved an action plan. I hired an experienced marketing analyst, Luiz Fernando Valente Machado, profoundly knowledgeable of the market in Rio de Janeiro. Together we determined places that I should go to as a regional manager so that we would be better known in the city and improve our performance. One of the key actions we took was to bring together the city's top business owners on a yacht to attend a lecture by economist and former Finance Minister Maílson da Nóbrega[9]. We took everyone for a cruise in Guanabara Bay, passing under the Rio-Niterói bridge, and offered a cocktail. We got 50 entrepreneurs on the yacht. It was early 2009, just after the mortgage crisis broke out in the United States, and it was in their interest to hear that lecture. We used all our creativity and were able to get closer to the people we wanted to relate to - with the benefit that no one could leave because they were all in the boat on the high seas. The event was a success, and the sales results were exceptional.

This need for adaptation happens all the time in the seller's life. Throughout my career, I have dealt with clients from different countries countless times, and there is no Brazilian state for which I have not sold. I always had to adjust to the different realities of each place, preparation that is part of the planning stage.

---

[9] Maílson da Nóbrega was Minister of Finance between January 1988 and March 1990. He reestablished relations with the international financial community after the 1987 foreign debt moratorium. Available at: http://mailsondanobrega.com.br/perfil/. Accessed March 8, 2019.

Recently, for example, as Director of Business Expansion at Algar Telecom, when we were opening the company´s operations in the Northeast of Brazil, I found out the importance of transmitting confidence to the decision maker when making the initial contact via telephone, to try to schedule a visit. Early on, I noticed a distrust on the part of potential customers who were concerned about who we were and how we had gotten their phone - perhaps because the market in the region is not as explored as in the Southeast where in common to receive calls from sales representatives all the time. My team learned that decision makers would not accept us until the seller clarified how we had gotten their contact. Understanding this difference in behavior has led us to adapt to approaches. We realized the importance of detailing how we got to the customer when we introduced ourselves before we even talked about our service.

A trip I made to China on business while authoring this book in November 2018 was yet another learning immersion. I tried to prepare myself as much as I could before talked to several people who had already been to China to understand what it is like to do business with the Chinese. I had completely different experiences there from what I am used to here. The presidents of the companies that I visited always sat facing me, who was the head of the Algar Telecom´s delegation, and the others around him positioned themselves according to the hierarchy. In conversations, the presidents just looked at me, as if the other employees were not there. When serving tea, in a traditional ceremony, the president always takes the first sip, followed by the others. There are specific rooms in the restaurants for business meetings - they do not negotiate in the open hall of the establishments, so people at the nearby tables do not hear the conversation. That is, there are several customs that, if not followed, disrupt business. Failure to follow them may not prevent a sale or partnership from happening (as my goal was on that trip), but it can make the process difficult and slow because you spend time apologizing and getting around delicate situations. In addition, the exponential seller does not have to waste this time and tries to shorten the path to sale as much as possible, considering all the factors that involve it - including, and adaptations to the potential customer's culture.

I have one more story that demonstrates how important this issue of culture is in the negotiations. I once had a meeting with a client of Arab origin, director of a large company. I did not know him, I went to the first visit, understood the demand, and came back with a perfect solution that met everything his company needed. The price was good and although he was pleased with the proposal, he did not close the deal with me. We had several business lunches, in which he was interested in knowing who I was in my personal life, asking everything I did or did not do. Over time, I realized that deep down, this client wanted to know if I was a good guy, given his values, or if my personal habits clashed with his culture. For this director, more important than the service I sold, was whether I was a trustworthy guy, a person he could shake hands with, and with whom to close a deal. Knowing this, I always tried to demonstrate, by gestures and words, that I was a serious, ruled salesperson and that he could trust me. And the client only closed when he felt safe about it.

I could write about countless other stories of interactions like these. I notice that even the client's gender usually influences the negotiation. Selling to women is different from selling to men. This is due to cultural factors, which may change over the years as women increasingly assume decision-making positions within companies. However, in my experience, women today are much more objective and harsher than men to negotiate.

So, before you visit, consider: who is the decision maker? What is your culture like? What is the origin of his company? In large groups, especially multinationals, you often need to negotiate with a foreign person. If you are going to a meeting with someone from another culture, be prepared for it too and win the sympathy of your client.

Learn Languages

As much as you sell only to domestic companies, knowledge of other languages, especially English, Spanish will undoubtedly bring you benefits and put you in a prominent position in sales. The world is increasingly globalized, product and service nomenclatures and information are often in English or Spanish, and negotiations with people of different nationalities are happening more often.

Once, for example, we were in Jundiaí, in countryside of São Paulo, Brazil, closing a big deal by Algar Telecom with a large Chinese company that provided services to Apple. The factory came to Brazil because the government had reduced the tax rate for those who produced smartphones here in the country. We tried to sell our telecommunications services, but we were surprised to lose the deal for a Chinese competitor, China Telecom. Why do I bring this example? Today we compete with the entire world. A company from China that does not even operate in Brazil sold a business to a Chinese company here. Those who are unprepared, unable to argue and argue in other languages will miss the opportunity.

On another occasion, we sold to a technology start-up company in Campinas, Brazil, that quickly became a global company. After a while, the founder, pleased with our services, came back to us, and said, "I need you to serve me in the United States and negotiate with the people there." They could have hired a US company directly, but they preferred that we find a solution for them. As we didn´t had telecom network in the US, we rented from a company that operates in that country to interconnect with our network. In this case, once again, the constant preparation of the sales professional is fundamental. There is no possibility of accommodating, considering serving only Brazilian companies, because today the markets are global. It is important to invest in English and other languages, such as Spanish and Mandarin, because if you do not prepare and an incredible opportunity arises, you will lose the sale.

Expand your repertoire

Being up to date and knowing what is happening in the country and around the world is also part of the cultural baggage expected of an exponential seller. Internal and external political factors and events influence your country and world economy all the time. They can cause currency fluctuations, for example, and affect both your customer's prices and market by changing buying decisions. You may not be able to visit China, but you must find out what is going on there, in the United States, in Europe, in Latin America. As a rule, this knowledge will be used when you negotiate with customers. Showing that you know what is going on in the world improves the arguments and provides security for the other party.

The salesperson must follow the news, be prepared to adapt to sudden changes in strategy and reinvent himself very quickly. When changes affect the market, it is important to be proactive, bring innovative ideas and possibilities to increase sales.

I was still working at Cabelte, in Portugal, when, between the late 1990s and the early 2000s, severe economic crises impacted business - which until then had been booming. I remember that it all started with a monetary crisis in Russia, followed by what became known as the "internet bubble[10]". The telecommunications market went into crisis and, unfortunately, the crisis reached my company. To make matters worse, our company had acquired dollar debt to settle in Brazil and, with the sharp devaluation of the Brazilian currency against the dollar in 2002, the short-term debt of the company more than doubled very quickly. My job was threatened. It was difficult to get new orders and the collapsing company did not even have the money to produce and deliver orders it had already received. That was the first big challenge I had to face in my sales life.

We created an action plan to operate in the face of these adversities. In partnership with my tutor at the time, Edson Riera, a very experienced salesperson, with whom I learned a lot (I will tell

---

[10] When the value of overvalued shares of technology companies, the so-called "dot-com", plummeted after a speculative burst.

you some of the lessons I learned from him on the following pages), I had the idea of going after customers and offering discounts to those who paid us in advance. With the money we received in advance, we bought the material to produce those orders and make the deliveries. We made this proposal to several customers. It was difficulty, but with that we guaranteed the delivery at least to those we had sold - because the exponential seller knows that, after the sale is made, the responsibility is yours until delivery (I talk more about this attitude in the chapter about after sales). Only in this way does it ensure that future sales happen.

This exit was only possible because we were attuned to world economic events and, consequently, what was happening in our market. We had strong and convincing arguments. Times of crisis require from the salesperson many movements, strategies, and competence. You need to understand the world around and get ready, as crises can happen at any time. If they do occur, it is necessary to look for alternatives, which require resilience and a lot of creativity. Not an easy posture for those already facing low sales and income - as commissions also fall at such times.

At that time, unfortunately, all our effort was not enough, because the company really faced a complicated financial situation. As soon as I noticed that circumstance, I left in search of a professional relocation. At the end of that year, I left the company, which broke down at the beginning of the following year.

In mid-2003, when I was still looking for new opportunities, once again my salesperson adaptation capacity was tested - in an unusual situation, but that sometimes happens with sales. I got the call from a colleague I had worked with at Cabelte. It was a proposal for me to sell a fiber-optic cable as early as the following week to a large telecom company that was expanding and needed to install a submarine cable under Guanabara Bay in Rio de Janeiro, Brazil. The cable would be made in the United States, and my job was to take two company's buyers to the manufacturer's headquarters in Boston to test the product in front of them (and make sure the quality was good). The problem is that although I had all the prerequisites to make the sale (USA visa, notions of English, international experience about fiber optic market), I knew absolutely nothing about submarine cables, and I had never sold the product and I had no idea how to make the test. My colleague told me that when I arrived in Rio (to take a flight to USA), some people would teach me how to test the cable before traveling to the US with potential customers.

I accepted the challenge. I went to Rio and had only two hours to learn how to do the test before going to the airport, where I would meet the two buyers that I would travel with all night. Still at the airport, I was fortunate enough to meet a person that was offering the submarine cable installation services with divers for my potential customers. This guy taught me a lot about how to install submarine cables and I got more knowledge and arguments to talk with my customers during the flight.

After a connection flight in Miami, we arrived in Boston and noticed the rush of customers to quickly test the cable and gain time to enjoy the city. Given this, I streamlined the process as much as I could to please them and increase my chances of success - as I often insisted throughout these pages, the sale is the result of a good relationship. Arriving at the manufacturer, I excused myself, and without the customers noticing, I saw the cable before calling them to take the test. At the end, everything was good: I tested it, and they bought it. I got a good commission, a very welcome money at that time when I was out of a steady job.

It may have seemed easy, but it was a painful and tense process. It was less than ten days between that call from my colleague and the deal. I had to sell something new to people I did not know before, without building any previous relationship. I remember I was very anxious; I had to think and act fast. I had to improvise to imply that I knew the product well - always within ethics and responsibility, of course. Situations like this are not so common in salesperson´s day but can happen. On another occasion, for example, I was in the middle of a conventional sales process, following my schedule, and the customer called me desperate, requesting me to change the order. Therefore, the salesperson also must be prepared to be able to meet these unforeseen events and seize unique opportunities to close a deal.

Market Research

Do you know deeply about your product or service, or is your knowledge superficial? Do you feel able to have a technical conversation with the customer about all aspects, features, and details of what you sell? If your answer is no, I am sorry to say that you are moving away from exponential sales. You must be prepared to answer any questions you have about the purchase, including technical and theoretical questions.

Digging deeper into the world of what you sell is necessary for any sales professional. Study all about the history and portfolio of the company you represent. Take a deep dive, understand the features and strengths and weaknesses of your product or service. As much as many salespeople rely on a technical professional's support to ask questions or make proposals, do not hesitate to ask them questions before you start selling and become an expert on the subject.

This is a recommendation that fits any professional in every area. A doctor, for example, always needs to be informed and up to date about his or her specialty, as patients often search Google in advance for a particular disease or symptom and come to the office with questions about what they read. The same goes with sales. It is the knowledge that provides confidence and security for the customer. The more informed you are in conversations and meetings, the more likely you conquered the buyer, anticipating steps to close the deal.

Any salesperson stands out by understanding well what they sell. In 2018, I had to travel to Porto Alegre, south of Brazil, to start the Algar Telecom´s operations in the city, and when I got there, I noticed that I had forgotten the cable to recharge my cell phone. I was walking in the city to study the market when I entered a store where I would find a recharger and I asked a salesperson for the cheapest one. What was not my surprise when the young salesperson gave me a real class about rechargers for my device! At the end, I was convinced that it was not worth buying the cheapest product, even for a short time, because it could cause loading problems. With convincing arguments, he proved that it was better for me to invest in an intermediate item, which, even without being the original (more expensive) one, had the use authorized by the manufacturer. Much of what the salesperson said I already knew, but he was so prepared that it surprised me and made me change my mind. When we opened the operation of the company in that city, I did not hesitate to get his contact to offer a job opportunity. This professional was hired and is with us currently. For a long time, he was our best salesperson in the Porto Alegre operation and consequently he received a promotion.

I mentioned this example to reinforce how knowledge is a sales driver, regardless of area of expertise. The salesperson in question was young and early in the sales career but prepared to understand what he was selling. When I walked into the store, he was ready to offer his best service, quickly identified my quality-minded profile, and, knowing that, sold me something different from what I went to buy.

How does your market work?

In addition to becoming an expert about your company, product, or service, it is important to understand how your overall market works. Research and study how your business segment is impacted by the macroeconomic conditions of the country. Is the segment in crisis or growing? What will be the market demand for your product or service? What are the trends for the future? Should innovative technologies or new products emerge?

Also, identify who your competitors are, what types of approaches they use with customers, and what results they get. To do this, anything goes: analyze marketing actions and competitive advertising campaigns, observe the expansion of brands (physically and online, in digital media), research on them on the internet, participate in industry events (such as trade shows and lectures) and approach professionals in the area to exchange experience with them. I have always participated in industry events and built a large network of contacts. Of course, no one will pass strategic information from your company to the competitor, but there is always an exchange of information that is beneficial to both sides. In these shares, I met good colleagues in the profession. When I left Cabelte and was out of work for a while, for example, I even made sales in partnership with a colleague who had been my competitor in the past.

Those who know little about the market should approach experienced people - inside or outside the company. Learning from our elders is crucial to career growth. Throughout my life, I have always had a mentor, an experienced person whom I admired, inspired, and received advice from. At first, these mentors were my parents, my aunt, and my uncles (the sellers). From the beginning of my sales career, I have always identified professionals who imparted knowledge to me. Even today, even as a director, I look for my mentors when I am in a tough time or need to make a crucial decision. I always have two or three people who advise me. Even though I have an intuition about the best way forward, I like to hear opinions from those I trust. They do not make the decision for me, but they help me make it. Therefore, I suggest that when you feel insecure, seek the knowledge and wisdom of those who have gone through similar paths. Sometimes the solution to what you need is in someone's experience. Do not suffer from the "I am the best; I know how to do it myself" syndrome.

When I was at the beginning of my career and working in Portugal for Cabelte, I had a terrible experience that might have been avoided if I had received and accepted some advice. As I told you, I made projects and proposals for sales. Once we were technically qualified to compete in a major competition to supply cables to a French company. We prepared everything. Our commercial manager at the time went to France several times, created a relationship, and made a good presentation of our company to the potential customer. We got all the details, such as the size of the cables and the technical details that gave us competitive advantages. As with all competition, the lowest price would win and, with so much information (much more than competitors), we were able to make the best offer. I worked hard on the proposal and did my best to get everything perfect, without gaps. We were sure we would win. I already dreamed of the glory of being a beginner and a Brazilian, having made such an important sale. However, we lost.

Competitors had to bid on a unit price for each material and multiply the total amount of the project. The competition was for the unit price. I do not remember the values, but at the end of opening the envelopes, our price was the lowest, but with one detail: among the companies that put the price. One of the competitors thought further and wrote in the proposal that it would make $

0.20 less per unit than the lowest price (it was private competition, and this strategy was allowed). It was a great frustration, because we lost a lot of time making the best proposal, and this competitor got the victory due to a simple insight. I did not think about the imponderable and, of course, hardly anyone would do it in the face of something extremely creative and aggressive. But who knows, if I had shown my proposal to someone more experienced, I would have been helped to go further and prevent failure. In sales, you must be prepared for everything. Many times, you need to look for creative alternatives, and this sale taught me that. If our company were prepared, we would think in advance of a way around the situation if a competitor offered a lower price than ours. We could prepare a cost structure for this and surround ourselves. But we were so certain that we would win that we were not prepared enough.

Much later, at Algar Telecom, I had the opportunity to apply the learning of this frustrating experience. My dream then, in mid-2005, was to sell to CPFL, a power distribution company in Campinas, Brazil. I would walk past the company's headquarters daily and think, "I want to sell to them, it will be a milestone for me." One day, this opportunity arrived: We entered a competition to sell telecommunications services to CPFL. It was a big competition, so relevant that it would enable the effective creation of a branch of my company in the city (I was still acting alone as a salesperson, without a set up structure, which happened in the future, and then I was promoted to manager). We competed with companies much larger than us and worked hard, in partnership with an engineer, to offer the best price and technical offer. However, I remembered the history of competition in Portugal and was aware of what could offer more to tie my offer well. In addition to setting the lowest possible price, I had the idea of offering a payment alternative. Every telecommunications company pays a fee to the power's companies for the use of their power poles for fiber optic cables (there is even a fixed price per pole). I knew how much my company payed for CPFL power poles and, in the proposal, I gave the option that the total values of that sale be reverted to rental posts. That is, we would provide the services in exchange for using the power poles. We won the competition and there was no need to use this alternative. Even so, this time, I gave no chance to the imponderable.

Know your potential customer in steps

As I said, knowing who you sell to and what that buyer is about are essential factors. However, until you reach the customer who will effectively close business with you, there is a long way to go. Primarily, you need to identify the universe of this potential customer base broadly and broadly and then find and approach the people who will buy from you. To do this, there are basic questions every salesperson needs to consider: who would buy what you sell? Are your audience companies or individuals? In the end, who makes the purchase decision for your product or service? What are the characteristics and profile of this decision maker? Why does he need your product or service?

As you identify your potential client, narrow the description. If you are a business, know what sizes (small, medium, or large) you can introduce yourself to, the industries that need what you sell, etc. Understand the market of these audiences, whether they are in crisis or not, and how relevant your product or service is to each of them. If you are an individual, find out details of these potential buyers, such as age, income, and spending habits.

This initial survey is what will guide your sales planning from then on. For example, in my case, as I work in the telecommunications market, I know that the service I offer is extremely relevant to the banking industry. If a financial institution does not have internet access these days, it does not work. For a shoe factory, network access may be relevant, but not to the point of stopping production if there is a temporary problem in the connection. Both are my potential customers, but the approach and selling points for each are different. You need to understand the relevance of what you have to offer to each audience, prioritize strategies, and plan specific approaches.

It is not always easy to reach this potential end customer. Here is another example: A few years ago, an aircraft company wanted to hire me to sell aircraft maintenance services. I was not interested, as I was happy with my job at the time, but I nevertheless explored this extremely customized segment to understand how it worked. I was informed by the contractor that the goal was to sell 30 maintenance services per month. Curious, I asked, "Who buys aircraft maintenance?" Behold, he answered me: "The buyer is the owner of the aircraft, but it is the pilot who strongly influences the purchase. This is because the owners of a plane are usually busy people who do not understand about maintaining it. The person who determines who does the maintenance is the pilot. Because of this peculiarity, the seller of that service had to look for the pilots to make the offer, not the owners of the aircraft.

In that case, the person who wanted to hire me had already done some good planning and had a list of pilots to look for if they accepted the job offer. It is at this point that the seller becomes aware of the conversion rate I mentioned on previous pages. At that time, I did not ask the contractor what the conversion rate was because he was not interested in the opportunity. But to make this issue clearer to those who still have doubts, if his goal were to sell 30 maintenance services a month, with a hypothetical two-to-one conversion rate, I would need to name 60 potential pilots to have a chance of reaching the goal.

Approach the potential buyer

Since you already have a list of potential customers to prospect (as I explained on previous pages), the seller needs to find out who to contact to schedule a visit. This is an especially crucial step in the planning process; often crucial to the success of the sale. You need to know who the decision maker is and how to access him / her to make the business approach. I strongly recommend that, at this moment, you strive to get that person's direct phone number.

If the prospect is a business, there may be a specific purchasing industry. Even so, I suggest looking for the person personally responsible for using what you sell - in most cases, it is this professional who influences the buyer to decide. Search directly for the manager responsible for the specific area that uses what you provide. A frequent misconception is that the seller looks for the wrong person and wastes time addressing whoever does not decide to buy. Of course, it is sometimes not possible to reach the decision maker, but before you are sure you will not be able to do it, do everything in your power.

You can use several tools to contact this person and schedule the visit. There are already established methods, such as acquiring mailings and conducting internet searches (on company websites and search engines). Today, with technology, there are many companies that sell ready-made database signups or artificial intelligence software. Buying mailings, for example, can sometimes be worth it because they bring in company data that is not available on the internet, such as postage and billing, and sometimes you can reach out to who decides to buy. These lists provide information that is helpful but should not be used as a direct mailing tool as this does not work for personalized sales.

However, do not limit yourself to buying mailings or be on one strategy. Think out of the box. Pay attention to your network, connect to your network, look for mutual friends, ask for directions, dare. Sometimes you come to a decision maker in unpredictable and informal ways.

Use and abuse social networks like Facebook, Instagram, Twitter, and LinkedIn to search. By 2019 at least, these have been invaluable channels for identifying potential customers and finding ways to reach them. In all these cases, you can use keyword searches from your target area or audience. I go back to the day when a LinkedIn business manager came to me to offer a company product because it demonstrates how effective these technology tools are. He found me through his own social network, because he did the search for directors of big companies.

A key factor to note is that he was not my connection but identified that we had a mutual friend. With this information, the account manager took advantage of an informal face-to-face meeting he had with our mutual friend to ask him for my WhatsApp number, so he approached me to arrange a face-to-face visit. Note that he did not do this through the social network.

I like this case very much because it demonstrates the right way for the exponential seller to use social networks to identify potential customers: they are just identification tools, not ways to effectively try to sell. It is for you to find opportunities or decision makers but not to close a deal.

There is another story that, on the other hand, reveals how not to act. I received, through social networks, the contact of a sales representative of a car rental company. He sent me an extensive standard message introducing himself, offering his services to Algar Telecom and trying to arrange a meeting with me. Obviously, I did not answer him. I only read your message because you were looking for an example of what not to do when authoring this book - otherwise you would never have known about it. Well, reflect with me: I am a director of a large company, my work schedule is full, and I do not have time to read messages from strangers via email or social networks. I get over 200 emails a day, ranging from important business conversations to product and service offerings. When I see that the issue is not relevant, I delete the email immediately - if I do that, other directors, or managers of companies, who are mostly buyers, also do the same. As much as these people may come to be interested in the offers, most of the time, the messages are deleted without even being read. This is a very weak, basic, and non-exclusive approach.

Social networks are important tools to stimulate customer search. They help in prospecting but are not for the consultative selling of personalized products and services, which is the focus of this book. In this kind of selling, where relationships with other people are needed, these tools are helpful, but what really makes a difference is the salesperson. Contacting through WhatsApp can work because the use of the tool is increasingly constant. But in general, you need to call to make an appointment. Introduce yourself, say what you came for, and politely ask if the person can welcome you to know what you have to offer.

Going back to my second example on this topic, what would be the recommended stance if a car rental seller were exponential? The first thing would be to do extensive research on the company I work for. Soon he would find out that this is a big company that rents a lot of cars. In fact, we are a potential customer for car rental, but by sending me an impersonal message, this professional immediately canceled the possibility of making the sale, because I ignored him and did not answer him. His correct posture would be to find my phone and call me. I noticed that we have 70 mutual friends on the social network where he approached me, which means that he could contact any of them, whom he is close to, and get my number. This is what the good sellers do: they use the online environment to search, but as soon as possible they get out of the virtual world and move on to personal contact. A proactive stance in this regard is critical. If this professional could not get my phone number, I could call the company I work for and try to talk to my assistant to make an appointment with me. Too naive of him to suppose that a large company would start a business through an impersonal message on a social network. Renting a corporate car fleet is extremely personalized. You need to have human contact, someone to explain the conditions of service and make a unique budget, considering the needs of the buyer. No one gets on the internet and, with one click, rents a thousand vehicles. Not to mention that the message from this seller was extremely standard. He sent the same text to everyone.

Using strategies like this is common when standard salespeople are looking for sales. They believe that by firing the same message at multiple potential customers, they are saving time. However, with that, we waste not only time, but opportunities.

Before I generate misunderstandings with what I just wrote, I want to point out that social networks can be good selling tools, but products and services that do not need a salesperson. I bought a jacket for my son through a social networks channel - but it was not a personalized product, because it was enough to choose the color, size and make the purchase.

Sometimes resorting to the classic method and knocking directly on the company door works. When I first joined Algar Telecom in September 2003, I had recently left Cabelte and the sector that I worked for (Optical Fiber Cable), was still in crisis. It was difficult to get a job when I received a call from a former co-worker with an invitation to join Algar's expansion team, which had just received authorization from Anatel (National Telecommunications Agency) to operate in Campinas.

I did not know anything about selling telecommunication services - until then, I only sold products for the industry - but my colleague encouraged me: "It's selling, and you understand that!" I agreed to participate in the selection and was hired on condition that I move to the Campinas region and be responsible for the start-up of operations in the city.

I open parentheses here to talk about the importance of the salesperson having family support. At the time, my wife, Leticia (the same one I tried to impress with tennis lessons), worked as a doctor in Sao Paulo and we had to make a whole arrangement in our life for the change. With sales, it goes like this: depending on the company, the professional travels a lot and the understanding of family members is fundamental to the success of the job.

As we moved, I heard the comment from my manager, Alexandre Crescenzi: "Our company has nothing in Campinas. This is your office, and this is your communication tool"- and handed me the corporate car key and a cell phone (a "brick" at the time). I also received a personal computer to take home.

I started operations in Campinas, Brazil, alone and from scratch, in a completely new segment for me. It was the period when I had to undertake the most in my life. I had to sell telecommunication services from an unknown company locally, with no identified prospects, relationships or contacts established. Besides this, I needed to make my first sale as soon as possible to begin operation in the city.

Both I and the company knew the importance of knowing very well what I was selling before venturing to find customers. So, the first thing I did was a weeklong immersion at Algar's headquarters in Uberlândia, Brazil where I got to know all the company's products and portfolio. Of course, technical knowledge increases over time, but knowing as much as possible about the company before joining it was indeed essential.

After that, the following week, when I arrived in Campinas to work, I thought: "Who do I know in this city? Who will I offer the product to?"

I ran my hand through my entire portfolio of contacts and remembered a fiber optic factory with whom I had already interacted in my last job. I looked for an old friend inside the company who gave me a hint: "There is a new manufacturer of electronic products in town called Texas Instruments that needs telecommunications services." I had no contact at this company, so I decided to knock on their door. I decided to go in person because I had my friends inside information. I knew that if I called, I would be transferred from extension to extension and could hear a negative because it is much easier to say "no" in the phone. In person, however, I would transmit confidence and security, paving the way for sale. I introduced myself to security at the concierge and not only found out who oversaw the area of Information Technology (IT), but this person agreed to receive me even without having scheduled the visit. They precisely needed a telecommunication service to link Campinas with the branches in Rio de Janeiro and São Paulo in Brazil.

No matter how hastily all was done, I had prepared for that sale. I knew my product well and researched what I could about Texas Instruments before looking for them (I already knew, for example, that they had units in Sao Paulo and Rio). Once there, I explained to the customer what I had to offer, gave him security, and at that moment, even without knowing Algar, he contacted me to the buyer, who wanted to talk about price. I did not even have a project, so I asked for it a few days - so I insist that custom selling is hardly done on the first visit. I came back a while later with the proposal, and the buyer asked for a discount. I still did not have the autonomy to lower the price alone, as I was new to the company. Immediately, I called my boss. Adrenaline was on the skin. Crescenzi was surprised that I was about to sell to a big company:

- Will you sell Texas Instruments? he asked excitedly.

- I am trying. Give me the price I sell! - I told him.

- This value has no condition ...

- I am in front of the buyer, give me the price now that I will sell.

- Okay, go ahead! he said, changing his mind, but still unbelieving.

I hung up the phone, gave the discount, and the buyer closed it. With this sale, Algar Telecom's operation in Campinas was opened with success, about 15 days after my hiring. It was a successful case, and I received the invitation to tell this case for other salespeople in the company's annual convention. It was an expressive sale that could be a motivation for others - which happened.

The importance of networking

I hope it has been clear so far how much a relationship network helps us reach potential customers and increase sales. In my history as a seller, there are countless occasions when I sold thanks to my contacts. We all experienced difficulties in this area. When I really wanted to sell to a particular company and could not reach anyone inside, I remembered that "there's always someone who knows someone who works where I want to sell." I would ask people and when I found a common contact, I would ask for help. Most of the time, colleagues give us strength.

I once wanted to sell to a large financial advisory firm and talked informally down the hall to my staff about the difficulty of reaching a decision maker within the organization. At that moment, an intern passed by us and, as I spoke loudly, listened to an excerpt from the conversation. Behold, the young woman came to me, saying that she could help, because her father was one of the partners of the company in question. And so not only was I introduced to her father, but I also took her to attend the meeting with him. I could never imagine that within my own team there was someone so close to the person I needed to talk to.

I was recently at a birthday party in my condominium's ballroom. The birthday man was one of the residents, who turned 40. Among the guests were the neighbors, family, and some colleagues of his work. As I am communicative, I made a point with a man who was by my side. I commented that I work at Algar Telecom, and before long he was asking me if we could offer a service for his company. I left my business card, and even though I was no longer a seller, I gave his contact to one of our sellers to look for him. Weeks later, the man called me saying he was well attended, had contract the service and was satisfied. In this telephone conversation, I learned that he had contact with people from a third company in the region I was seeking to approach. Quickly, this customer referred me, and I opened the way for another sale.

Even the roadside restaurant where I had breakfast when I was a salesperson in countryside of São Paulo, Brazil, was the stage for me to close business. I frequented the restaurant daily to have my coffee before work. One of these mornings, I met an education executive whom I had sought in the past to offer services, but we had not closed a deal. He also had a habit of having breakfast at this same restaurant, where we would eventually meet and talk about amenities. One day he told me that he needed to talk to me, because the broadband provider they had contracted was not delivering the service on time. The education network was booming, and they needed a non-failing provider. I was introduced to the president of the company, which at the time was Anhanguera Educacional (today Kroton, the largest education group around the world), and we signed a contract with them. I even remember that it was a risky sale because the demand was so high, and we needed to plan well to be able to meet them. It worked. We served all new sites on time, were called to supply services to each inaugurated school and our company grew up with them. All thanks to a roadside coffee.

"Selling is the art of relationship"

There is a maxim that, while cliché, can never be ignored: "Selling is the art of relationship." Anyone who proposes to be a salesperson needs to like people and relationships. If you are a professional salesperson, you will necessarily have to develop this skill. Otherwise, you will lose business opportunities. Also, be proactive: It does not matter if you only sell to businesses. Regardless, selling always happens from human to human, no matter how much the buyer represents an organization. Basic relationship issues matter when closing a deal. I will talk more about this in the second part of this book, when I approach the execution step.

So, when it comes to finding where your customer is, do not hesitate to trigger your network, ask for help and directions.

Reinforcement: There is always someone who knows someone who knows the customer you want to prospect. Search for these shortcuts, shorten paths. An exponential seller must always use this feature. Imagine how paralyzing it is to look at a list of companies to approach, calling at the general extension without being able to talk to anyone! If you do not have the decision maker's phone at hand, move, probe your network. If you do not remember anyone, use social networks to find common connections. The access we seek may come from the least imaginable.

Also, keep an eye on your day-to-day life and do not miss business opportunities - they can come from your condominium neighbor's birthday party. We are constantly relating to people who may need what we have to offer. Do not waste opportunities. I photographed the following sentence on the door of a room at the Ohio University Sales Center, where I got my MBA degree: **"Nothing Happens Until Somebody Sells Something" by Ralph Schey**[11]. We are selling or buying something all the time, and the exponential seller is aware of it.

---

[11] Ralph Schey was CEO and President of Scott Fetzer and followed and funded sales education at Ohio University, USA. The Sales Center was founded in 1997 and, in 2006, for the generosity of the Schey family, it was named Ralph and Luci Schey Sales Center. Source: https://business.ohio.edu/about/centers-institutes/the-schey-sales-centre/about-us/ Accessed April 8, 2019

"See with the hands"

While networking, search engines, social networks, databases, and artificial intelligence software are all valuable tools to help us prospect clients, in some situations it is important to use good old field research. I learned from Weber Pimenta, former president of Algar Telecom, the expression "see with the hands," which summarizes this process very well. How do you "see with your hand"?

In 2010, I received an invitation from Algar Telecom to be regional sales director for São Paulo state. I took over with the mission of approving the company's expansion to five new cities in São Paulo state in a week. At the time, I had already learned a lot from the company about how to make a business plan and get approved for an investment. To do this, once again, I repeat: you need to study hard (as with any sale, in this case I was selling a project for my own company). In previous years, at Algar Telecom, I had learned to make a business plan with a top professional, for whom I was trained. So, when I needed to prepare for expansion into five cities in countryside of Sao Paulo, I already knew the way to the success: I studied and prepared myself with socioeconomic data and research on the regions, identified market potentials, made growth forecasts for cities and how much these investments would return to the company. However, I did not just believe in the statistical data: I also went "see with my hand." We took a car and drove to each of the cities to get to know the local market in person, how many companies existed and where each one was.

What does an action like this show us that is not in spreadsheets? Often the data is out of date. Visiting the sites points to effectively real business opportunities. At that time, we crossed what we gathered on the street with statistical data and set up an extremely accurate business plan. More recently, in 2018, as Algar's business expansion director, I was assigned to design a new expansion plan for other Brazilian regions. We did all the planning based on demographics using the existing theoretical portfolio. However, before we invested, I went to see all the cities once again, "with hands." There were regions where the statistical data did not indicate the concentration of companies and, during the visit, we identified that they were there. In other neighborhoods where spreadsheets indicated investment, we found several closed companies. Statistical data is not online or updated in real time (at least not yet when I authored this book). "See with the hands" therefore corrects these theoretical distortions.

You must also be entrepreneurial when making a sale. Going personally to a region where you believe your target audience is and exploring it well is part of it. Go to the place, talk to potential customers, find out their quirks and needs. Often, doing a computer-only study is not enough, especially if you are relying on statistical data or ready-made mailings. If this is your reality, personally visit the region before scheduling the visits, so as not to be negatively surprised later.

It is also important to make sure that the potential customers you are listing to prospect are already loyal to your competitor. In that job offer I received to sell aircraft maintenance services, for example, before visiting potential pilots, it would be important to find out if each of them already has a maintenance service with which they are satisfied. If so, it would not be worth the visit as it would be a great waste of time. This check, therefore, can and should be done via telephone before the visit takes place.

It is important to understand where the customer is, the exponential seller acts proactively in finding, contacting, and approaching potential customers to offer a product or service and close a deal.

Schedule visits efficiently

Did the potential customer accept to receive you? Congratulations! The first step towards realizing your dream has just been taken. However, again you need to plan every move from now on. Have you ever wondered how tiring it can be to visit distant customers on the same day?

The salesperson needs energy, being emotionally good at the time of sale and organizing their work schedule. Never schedule visits at random.

The reality of how to accomplish this logistical task is one for every salesperson. Geographic factors influence a lot. Your potential customers may be distributed both throughout the country and only in your neighborhood. Therefore, it is necessary to analyze the potential market and outline the best strategy. This is not such a simple equation to make. Good planning, therefore, is especially important because there is a deadline to be met and a minimum number of prospects to be done within it to achieve the goal. All this must always be very well evaluated and organized.

Suppose you have customers across Brazil. Obviously, you will not catch a plane one day to Minas Gerais state, the next day to São Paulo state and the third day to Amazonas state. This goes for everyone, establish the best agenda. If in your case the potential market is in the same city, it is smart to work district by district. Think about one region each time. Do not schedule visits throughout the city at the same time, as this will waste your time - especially if you are in a big city with heavy traffic and traffic jams.

In some cases, the person who does this work of organizing the visits is the salesperson himself, especially if he works for a small business or is alone in a new unit, as it was my case for a few years at Algar Telecom in Campinas, Brazil. In addition, the sales professional will have a person to assist you, such as an assistant. Whatever the case may be, you will need to be well organized to meet the visits within the deadline.

When I was still working at Cabelte and was promoted to salesperson, I had the help of a good team, who supported me in my business proposals and collaborated a lot in the coordination of my visits. Sometimes I would go out and spend a month traveling from customer to customer. The professional who helped me made the phone calls and set up my entire schedule. I traveled from Rio to Sao Paulo, from Sao Paulo to Brasilia, from Brasilia to Recife, and so on. This routine required proper planning so that I had time to visit each client efficiently. There was a time when I needed to bring new consumers to the company portfolio, so I made a real pilgrimage all over Brazil. To this end, I applied everything I have been writing so far: I did not choose the destination regions at random, but through surveys of potential buyers. Since I worked with fiber optic cables, my focus was on telephone companies, power distribution companies, contractors (they bought cables because they signed contracts where they already supplied this product in the enterprises).

At Algar Telecom, when I was a regional manager in Rio de Janeiro, Brazil, an important logistical decision I made improved our performance. Those who know Rio know that the conditions of displacement from the central region to Barra da Tijuca are unfavorable. Our headquarters were downtown, and salespeople took over an hour to get to Barra da Tijuca, where, ironically, were our biggest customers. This difficulty got in the way of sales, so I decided to set up an office in Barra da Tijuca and hired salespeople who lived there to stay there - they only came to the central office once a week for meetings. In the other days, instead of spending time in traffic, they would sell. With this, we increased sales. In the end, the increase in company performance compensated for the extra cost of the new office.

Prepare for the first visit

Getting a first visit is a good sign, because it means the potential customer gave you the chance you needed and is willing to listen to you. As I pointed out, a good sale can require countless visits, and you need to know the purpose of each one. As we are still talking about the first personal meeting at this stage of planning, go with your prepared speech, considering the specifics and particularities of each client.

You can also schedule another visit to an old customer to introduce a new product or service. In this case, planning is even easier and more customizable because you already know its particularities and you do not have to introduce yourself again. In another example, you can visit someone who has already made a purchase just to find out if everything is in order with the order (I will talk about it in customer care) - yet your intention is to serve it well so that it comes back. to buy from you in the future.

So, do not forget: Before the first visit, thoroughly research the company, its market, and prepare the presentation and approach. The exponential salesperson is already at the first prepared meeting and with an initial idea of what he can offer the customer, but it is in the conversation that he discovers his real needs, a topic that I discuss deeply in the execution part. When a salesperson plans well and comes to the visit believing in what they sell, inspired by their Moonshot, their chance of success increases.

Create needs and opportunities

One thing is fact: sometimes the customer does not know what he needs and who tells him that the seller is. A good sales professional, knowing the business of the potential customer, creates the need and reveals it on the visit. Most of the time, this is something to be thought of in the planning stage before the meeting, because if you fail to produce a great idea when visiting the client, it may not appear. It is a great advantage to think ahead because you anticipate scenarios and surprise the buyer.

The idea is to think of everything the potential customer may need before the visit. Whatever you can think of beforehand is helpful and avoids wasting time negotiating both yours and the other person.

By the year 2000, I was still working at Cabelte and had been promoted to commercial manager. The fiber-optic cable market was still hot - before the aftermath of the dot-com crisis - and I realized that in addition to selling the cable, our company could sell bundled services. I analyzed which customers used the cables at construction sites outside the cities and realized that one way to present a differential in selling was to offer cable delivery directly on site. Until then, we delivered the products to the storerooms, and the buyers did the distribution on their works. With this solution of bundling the delivery service, sometimes I could not get to the competitor's cable price, but it created an advantageous differential (on-site delivery) and could even charge more because, by the buyer's accounts, it was worth it. I spoke to the company's CEO, Afonso Rodrigues, and managed to convince him to buy trucks to do the job. It worked very well, and we started to deliver to remote locations, making life easier for the customer and offering a solution he did not even know he needed. I created a need that did not exist in the market at the time. Today this is common, but no one delivered directly to work at that time. This creates a competitive advantage that is hard to compare. A while later, I still had a second idea: selling the service already with the cable installation, another need that companies did not know they had. With these and other strategies, we sold so much that, at a certain point, we eventually consumed all the factory capacity in Brazil, to the point that we need to import from Portugal to cover what we were selling.

Creating opportunities requires an entrepreneurial streak from the salesperson, because this kind of personalized selling is often referred to as a consultative sale, precisely because you give your client advice. You must unravel even what he does not know he wants. Always think about what you can do differently to sell more.

This kind of entrepreneurial vision can happen on a first visit to a new customer, but I understand that it is rare. It is easier to create needs when the salesperson is aware of the dynamics and operation of his market. I was only able to offer cable delivery myself when I worked at Cabelte, because I had already visited numerous clients and identified the movement to the point of creating a solution. Even so, there are situations where it is possible to propose something new from the first contact. Suppose you are used to selling to the pharmaceutical industry and know the pains and problems of this market well. When it comes to visiting a potential client in this industry, you can try to surprise the buyer and foresee a need they do not even know they have based on their competitors' record of accomplishment. You may even say that you have identified such a need because of your experience in the business.

Imagine now that you have scheduled a visit with an old customer and will find him or her to make an additional sale to reach your goal. Do you agree that you will have an advantage over this type of buyer? Because you already know your customer, have a relationship with him and often know details of the company, how it operates and the most critical sectors. This prior knowledge can help you identify a new need for the customer.

I give a hypothetical example considering my business, which offers telecommunications services. Suppose I have a customer to whom I have already sold a basic product, such as an internet link that has improved the performance of his business. Later, I learn that the customer made investments in his plant, which increased the level of production. With that, I can make a second visit to offer another service in my portfolio - in this case, a product that transmits real-time information to improve performance management and efficiency. With that, I create a need that the customer did not even know it had. At this planning stage, thinking about these possibilities before visiting is essential. Ponder: What else can you offer the customer to further improve their business or life?

Anticipating scenarios is also dependent on the complexity of the industry you will sell to. Imagine this: The market for the company you want to sell to is in crisis. One idea is that you already think of a differential to offer, so that it can overcome the difficult moment. It can be something like proving that your product is cheaper, and, with the economy, the company will reduce costs, or that it will bring more agility to production, putting it ahead of competitors. The solution will depend on what you have to offer: what matters most is the argument to be used to prove how you can help the customer overcome this difficult market moment.

In 2004, for example, I studied the newspaper market to sell to a regional newspaper. I knew the industry was in crisis when I offered them a swap: our internet services in exchange for ads. How did I anticipate this information? I had a history of the segment from accumulated experiences selling to this industry. I knew that the scenario was difficult, and that the newspaper was losing to electronic media. Thanks to this prior knowledge, I was able to anticipate a need and offer a proposal that was good for both sides: My company was new in the city and needed to promote its services in the region and, in parallel, the newspaper needed an internet connection. I proposed the exchange for a year and if they were satisfied with our services, they would pay for the plan. Said and done: After a year, the exchange was over, and they renewed with us.

But it was not just this argument that I used. I was completely prepared. I argued that the newspaper would gain production agility if it hosted all its content in a data center for data storage. This would allow any journalist to have online, remote, and simultaneous access to the files and programs used to produce the newspaper. The customer would never have imagined this possibility if I had not offered it. This is creating a demand for something the customer does not even know they need.

Reinforcement: Creating needs and opportunities is not so simple. It requires a lot of study and in-depth knowledge of each potential customer. The strategy becomes more effective the more the salesperson is prepared from the point of view of knowledge and experience. A new or inexperienced salesperson gets a little harmed at this stage because they do not have so much baggage on the market, but that does not mean they cannot think about it and try to anticipate it maximum the customer needs before first visit.

The exponential seller recognizes your limitations and looks for ways to overcome them. If you don´t have much knowledge about your market, you may want to look for experienced colleagues or pairs who are willing to share what they know. The important thing is to explore ways and never stop learning. In addition, seeking experiences with people who have been through a particular situation is always valid for both the new and experienced salesperson.

Sales path is not straight

I cannot finish this part of the planning without making an important note: You may do all your research, but do not identify enough audience to prospect, that is, not find the required number of names with the profile you want within your area to reach your goal. If this happens, what to do?

It is important to keep in mind that any distortions may exist along the way to the sale which, I am saying, is always not straight. Most of the time, the trail to effectively closing a deal has several detours. The salesperson must be prepared as he may go the wrong way and need to go back a few steps to find the right one. It should be noted that during planning, various assumptions, multiple targets to shoot your arrows should be considered. You must have choices of companies, segments, markets, and customers. If you think of only one way and it does not work, you will not make the sale and therefore will not reach the goal.

If you find that you have no market to reach the goal, look for solutions to reverse this scenario. I say this because it is almost inconceivable for any salesperson to come to the boss and say, "Look, I have no market to make this goal that you gave me. Could you review the goal for me?

As I have already explained, the goal is properly calculated considering the company's business ambitions. Also, as I have already discussed, what must be considered behind this number is not a simple sales goal, but an important personal dream to achieve, a moonshot, and selling the calculated value is necessary to achieve the purpose of your life - you cannot give up on it, as that is out of the question.

Instead, review strategies and renegotiate agreements with the company. There are strategies that can be taken to work around obstacles that come your way to sales. Sit down with your manager, and together talk about the goals, think of solutions. Bring in positive arguments to say that you really want to reach the goal, but you need favorable conditions for that. It is possible, for example, to seek more areas of activity (expanding locations to increase potential customers), to propose to enter a new business segment, to request to increase its product portfolio, to request authorization to work with discounts or to do something which is not yet allowed, but that could bring results and improve conversion rate. These are just a few examples of how important planning is. The unplanned seller cannot argue that way. He may even strive to reach the goal even without having a market, but eventually he will be frustrated for failing, even at the risk of losing his job.

My experience shows that, with rare exceptions, there is always a way around the lack of markets to work. When I was given tough but consistent goals, I had a stance of instead of saying I could not do it, asking for something more from the boss to achieve value. When you ask for help, you usually get it, because it is in everyone's interest in the company that you hit the stipulated amount. The important thing is to keep it in mind: the goal is the goal and once set, does not back down.

I once received a goal that seemed unreachable. My director said he needed me to triple the value of my sales and arranged a meeting on the issue in two days. I strongly followed my "personal mantra" of not fighting the goal, because I knew it would suit my dreams and purposes. I thought a lot about those 48 hours. On the day of the meeting, I claimed that the new goal was extremely challenging and made a request: "So that I can fulfill it, I would ask you to increase our product portfolio. With the current items, I cannot achieve the expected result, but if we increase, I am able. "At the time, I only had an internet link to sell, but I argued that if the company invested in offering voice links and other data products, it would be possible to triple the value of sales, as my boss had asked me. As I was a market research salesperson, I knew all the competitors offered those products. He accepted my suggestion because the company needed to grow. They quickly put new products in the portfolio and, with more options to offer customers, I hit the target within months.

On another occasion I was already a manager and noticed that I needed to increase the efficiency of my sales force. We found through benchmarking that our salespeople were 50% less efficient than our competitors - that is, if each of our salespeople sold $ 10,000 per month, competitors would get $ 15,000 for the same product line. I did not want to be inferior, and I set goals of $ 15,000, but a group of salespeople came to question me. They claimed that the increase was 50% and could not be achieved because there was no market. I asked them to forget the "crying", which had no conversation, because the competitors already did. I argued that if the others out there could do it, they could too, because they were better than them, because if they were not, they would not be there. The entire team was encouraged to think of ways and alternatives to increase sales by 50%. They followed and then produced some requests. I remember one of the requests was to increase staff to help schedule visits. Gradually solutions came along, and we managed to hit our new goal.

Do not skip planning

You, dear seller, as you read all the topics I dealt with at this stage of planning, have thought something like, "What a waste of time, why does all this work? It is better to go out selling right away, that I gain more time!" Believe me, as

121

tempting as it is to "skip" the planning phase and move on to execution you will move unprepared and lose time with reworks in the next phases.

Remember: The preparation period is essential and indispensable for you to get the best sales done, in the shortest time and in the best possible relationship. Note that a lot of effort is required for this. It is a mistake to think that the sale begins on the visit: it starts much earlier. If you go straight to execution, contact the customer, and make a proposal without planning in advanced, your chances of success are reduced. In this scenario, you may not sell well, sell what the customer does not want, and thereby not achieve your goal.

You may also find that every salesperson is already doing his best to hit and exceed goals to achieve his personal dreams, but nothing is that simple in everyday life. I agree and understand that the process is not easy and requires much resilience. I am not promising here a magical formula for success. However, what I can guarantee you is that if you ignore the planning, your chances of selling exponentially will be much lower unless you are lucky. But counting on luck is too risky for those that depend on the commission. Better to rely on technique and preparation.

The same reasoning goes for everything in life. For example, many people advise smokers to kick their addiction as it is bad for their lungs and their whole body. At such times, we often hear arguments like, "My father smoked until he was 90 and never had a problem with his lungs." True, this can happen, but the risk of health problems affecting smokers is much higher. We cannot handle cases by exceptions.

In sales, it is the same thing: Of course, there may be an unplanned over-the-top salesperson who goes around selling only with a good lip. But this is rare. And no matter how lucky you are, this preparation will certainly make your results even more effective. As one famous quote from American golfer Tiger Woods goes, "The more I train, the luckier I am"[12]. The more I dedicated myself to the sales career and studied about it, the better I got and the more I sold. Knowing where I wanted to go, having a moonshot, was a prime factor in that.

The salesperson who is unwilling to do all this automatically enters an endless negative cycle: he is not prepared and is always thinking that the goal is too high. The result is average sales, little experience of success and unfulfilled dreams. Frustrated and unmotivated, this professional sells even less. Planning reverses this logic. It makes the salesperson find his internal motivation, grow more as a professional, strengthen his network of contacts, learn, and gain new experiences. With this, your chance of

---

[12] The English phrase is "The harder I practice, the luckier I get" and would have been said by another famous golfer before being used by Tiger Woods. In the research I did, the origin is somewhat controversial, having been attributed to both Gary Player and Arnold Palmer.

success is much greater. This person also has a lot more repertoire for the following opportunities, which generates better results and, consequently, will promote a virtuous sales cycle. Good salespeople know it is worth spending some of their time planning because it ensures greater sales efficiency.

This situation reminds me of the following anecdote: two people were walking quietly through the woods when suddenly a bear appeared. One of them stops and starts putting on a sneaker. The other runs barefoot and, surprisingly, claims: "Why do you wear this? Do you really think it will be faster than the bear like that? Behold, the first one answers, "I don't need to run faster than the bear, I just need to overtake you." The exponential seller is like the character wearing sneakers. Of course, this person wasted time tying his shoelaces, while the other one already ran off. But he was better prepared for that situation and more likely to survive the risky situation.

How long does it take planning?

There is no rule or standard ratio of how much time a salesperson should spend planning your job, because selling is not an exact science. However, from my experience in the area, it is convenient to set aside at least 15% of your time for this. But I say: this is just an estimate, based on my own experiences. The important thing is that you study and test what works for you. There are exceptional and very experienced salespeople who plan everything mentally, for example, and may take less time than that. The important thing is to get to the execution already having a clear strategy for the sale.

The exponential seller ends the plan knowing what he wants. By the end of this work, a refined list of potential customers is already scheduled to visit. And you must get everything ready for the next step. Do everything not to waste time later and shoot the target at the time of execution.

To recap the planning step

In this first part, I talked about the steps that involve preparing the seller before going on the visit. This means having a moonshot, a dream or purpose behind sales.

I addressed the need to calculate this dream at the tip of the pencil and represent it in a feasible number.

I noted the importance of knowing how much to sell to achieve the expected result within the set time limit.

I later said that you need to find out who you will sell to (your target audience, your customer base), specifically map out who your prospects are and identify where they are located.

From there comes the time to thoroughly investigate who decides to purchase, schedule visits strategically and define the purpose of each one.

I stressed the importance of seeking to anticipate creative solutions, see opportunities and meet needs that the customer does not even think they have.

I emphasized how advantageous it is to always study, have cultural background and be informed to improve your repertoire in conversations and negotiations.

Finally, I talked about having resilience to recalculate routes if necessary and never skip the planning stage if you want to sell exponentially.

Part 2 - The Discipline of Execution

Imagine the following scene: You, the **seller,** have arrived prepared to visit your prospect. You have done all the research, have anticipated as much as you can about who you will talk to and the needs they may have. You have prepared your material and know what you are going to show. From now on, what is the best course of action to increase your chances of success?

The sale execution begins on the first customer visit. It is the period of relationship and negotiations before effectively closing the deal. In it, the salesperson performs everything he planned in the previous step. In a quick dictionary search, synonyms appear to perform, make, do, and fulfill verbs. And there is no better way to translate this step than these words.

As I have said a few times, selling personalized products or services will not be closed on the first visit. As a rule, on the first date, the salesperson knows your potential customer's demand, understands what they need, introduces you and your portfolio, and leaves with the mission of coming back soon with an attractive proposition.

The sale will not happen at the second meeting either. It may be, but in my experience, this is rare. In the second conversation, the buyer usually receives the proposal, asks questions, agrees to analyze it and, in most cases, asks for adjustments that the seller could not anticipate. The seller then returns home, changes the proposal again, based on the meeting, and goes to a third meeting, which this time has a higher closing potential. However, there may be the fourth, fifth, or sixth visits before the contract is signed. There are no rules. The complexity of what you are selling is what dictates the timing of the process - at the closing stage, I talk about how to realize when it is time to end the meeting cycle and pressure the client to decide.

Moonshot inspires your discipline

I call this phase of discipline of execution because, without being disciplined, the salesperson will not be able to perform what he or she planned to perform. Sometimes it is boring to fulfill all that has been previously defined. If you have established that you must make five visits a day to meet your goal, you must have the commitment and responsibility to make those five visits. You can face hard days: or you're lazy, or it is hot or cold, it is jammed, it rains, you are not well emotionally. But do it. Follow what was proposed in your planning.

Most of the time, as I said, the first visit is about business development, representation of your company, presentation of your product or service. Relationships with clients may not be easy, it requires patience, emotional preparation, and a lot of flexibility. Your initial idea may go wrong, the caller may not be on a good day, give you the expected attention, or demand much more than you anticipated.

Whatever the difficulty, be prepared to do what you commit to by setting the purpose of each visit. Doing so requires a capacity that I will reinforce a few times from now on resilience. We cannot meet all the goals first, most of the time we need to come back and reschedule. But do this: come back, plan again, fulfill with dedication and patience what you set for each client. Therefore, I say that discipline is required. Resilience really is the secret of execution, a factor that differentiates average salespeople from exceptional salespeople.

I will talk about moonshot again, which guides the good salesperson. The exponential salesperson stands firm in the face of difficulties midway through because he or she grounds his or her personal goals to close each deal. Knowing where to go is a crucial factor in not giving up. This helps you to be motivated, excited and resilient, important characteristics for those who always deal with people.

The power of attention

The exponential seller prioritizes the quality of the trade rather than hurrying to close soon. This is the great differential that I try to point out from the first pages of this book. The entire process is careful. First you study, plan, prepare, schedule the visit. Research even more about the client before meeting him. Care continues from now on during the execution of the sale. You must be considerate of the person who has agreed to receive it, understand what they need, and not push them to buy quickly or at any cost. This attention generates two things: the possibility of making a proposal and, consequently, a second visit, which is when you will submit this proposal. See how you can go about this.

As it is unlikely that the sale will be closed on the first visit, after that the seller asks for a deadline to design the buyer a solution that fits what he needs. Even if this adaptation is simple, you should formulate a specific proposal for the customer to feel valued and make sure that you are offering them the best possible solution that meets their needs at that time. Always think about what customization you can do. Sometimes the customer feels so special that you have put together a custom proposal for him that the price factor even disappears from the game, because he has already felt embraced by what was offered. It was all so individualized that he has no way of comparing him to his competitor. You made a deal for him.

The more the proposal is thought in this direction, the greater the chance of success. The time it will take for the second meeting varies with the client, their urgency. Of course, you will need a period to prepare something that meets his needs but try to keep it as short as he has asked. Design a proposal that fits exactly what the buyer needs, like Lego pieces, and get ready for the second visit.

In presenting what you have prepared according to my experience, it is also not recommended to be anxious to close the deal quickly. I suggest you be very didactic in explaining your solution. Sell it very well, safely, explaining that you designed everything especially for that customer. Show the customizations made by thinking exactly what he needed. It is important to show flexibility and make it clear that if he does not like something, you can change it quickly. It is time to be explanatory, flexible, show the possibilities, benefits, advantages, and gains that the buyer will have with the solution designed. Only at the end of the conversation should you talk about price. You "must avoid the price war during the game" and sell your solution by showing its benefits.

I have a story that illustrates how much personalization and customer care make a difference when closing a deal. When I was still sales manager of Algar Telecom, I had to hire cleaning services for our office, which was on the

11th floor of a commercial building. I remember very well that the salesperson of the company that provided this service for offices on other floors came to me, arguing that he was already in the building. I received it because I would really need to hire someone, and his company was already mobilized in the building. He brought the proposal, but his price was higher than other companies I had sought. As a buyer, I asked what his differential would be, because I could not afford more for the same thing, just because he already serves other customers in the same building. The salesperson returned on his second visit with a proposal, at no extra charge, to have a heavier office cleaning every weekend, in addition to the basic service already done from Monday to Friday. By offering it, he stepped out of the price game and showed me the benefits I would have from closing with him. In that case, it was a cleaner office, and I bought it. His services were a little more expensive, but it was worth it. Of course, if it were much more expensive, I would not close, but his offer was more comfortable and effective, and I thought it was worth paying a little extra for it.

What you as a seller need when submitting a proposal is to convey that credibility. The buyer must believe you, see that they are making every effort to offer you the best solution, and that it will really solve their problem. The format that the proposal is presented with should also be thought up carefully. It is advisable to put together an interesting and attractive presentation (with software that allows you to create custom slides or print on paper). I always printed two copies of the proposal and asked the other person to follow the information sheet by sheet, as I explained. Often, I would take a technical expert with me to give even more credibility to what was being offered.

Transparency: A Priority

Whenever I visit a client, I reinforce to myself, mentally, that I be as transparent as possible in that meeting. Before starting any conversation, I think: "I will be transparent. I have studied, prepared, know what this person needs, and I will not fool him."

I learned the importance of being honest and transparent with the customer as a child. As I revealed at the beginning of this work, my favorite play when I was a child was "pretending to be a salesperson." Around my 11 years old, I lived in a condominium with about 400 houses in Castilho, Brazil. A newspaper vendor appeared there, and many residents signed up, including my father. One day I went with him to the supermarket butcher shop inside the condominium, and Butcher Amauri asked him, "Mr. Salomon, don't you have an old newspaper in your house to bring me?" At the time, it was common to wrap the meat in newsprint (with the plastic underneath, of course). When I got home, my dad told me to take the newspaper to the butcher and keep the coins. I quickly produced the idea of collecting old newspapers of the neighbors, selling it to Amauri and getting some money. I went from house to house asking for an old newspaper, taking it to the butcher, who weighed everything in the balance and paid me every week. Once I realized that the wet paper was heavier, I purposely wet some, putting it in the middle to hide them. Amauri bought it and did not even notice it, but I felt so smart that I got home and told my dad all the proud strategy, as if it were an achievement. Of course, he got terribly angry, scolded me, saying it was wrong, that he had not raised me to do that. I remember very well my father pulling me by the hand and dragging me to the butcher shop to apologize to Amauri (I remember his name to this day because of this scene). Then I had to provide a free newspaper for a month. So, I learned that anyone who wants to succeed in sales must be honest and transparent. We cannot break the trust bond with the customer at the time of sale.

I carried this learning forever. Naive as the situation may seem, the message fits perfectly into any business relationship. To this day, I sometimes come across a situation where I could fool a customer, make a "little mistake" to sell more, but that memory comes to me automatically. As a manager or director, I had the experience of seeing a salesperson on the team trying to do the same to hit the goal, and I always call their attention. I do not do it simply because I am good, but precisely because I think about selling more. If we break the bond of trust, the deceived person will remember the fact forever.

As a result, we lost the customer and still have a bad reputation in the market. The exponential seller cares about your name because that is what he or she carries in the business relationship. This is what makes your sales cycle continuous and successful.

I have one more childhood learning in this sense that I carry with me to this day. As a child, I realized that there was no car wash in our small town. The residents of the condominium were washing their cars in other cities nearby. I did not hesitate to invite a friend to offer our neighbors a car wash together. When we saw that the car was dirty in the garage, we would ring the bell and ask to wash the vehicle. We even had a price list: the cheapest service was just washing. The intermediary included washing and vacuuming internally. Already the full service was washing, vacuuming, and waxing up. One resident had a large pickup truck, which was heavily soiled with mud, and on one occasion I offered to wash and vacuum her car, and she accepted. In the end, I saw that there were a few scratches and asked if I could wax up too, which she accepted. When I went to charge, I gave the value of the full service, but the customer found it expensive. I justified it because of the wax up, but she did not agree and paid me a lot less. I felt quite offended and angry, as if it were a mendicant, and I took a completely wrong attitude, which I am ashamed of today: I tore the note in front of her. That made a big fuss, I got a huge scolding from my mother, which, as my father had done the other time, made me apologize to the neighbor for my act. From that occasion, I carry the learning of the importance of clearly combining values with the customer always before the service is performed, explaining what is included. That day I remember that I explained to my mother that I had told the resident that the value was more expensive with the waxing up, but my mother insisted that it was my fault because if the client had not understood then I did not make the correct form. "You must talk in a way she understands. If she does not understand, you are wrong, she said. Of course, the biggest scolding was about my reckless act of tearing the money: "You can't rip money, because if you do that, you'll get arrested, got it?" She repeated.

From this story I learned not to speak half the words, to be clear and to specify very well what is included in each proposal. All of us salespeople go through times when we have the opportunity to make a "soft, light trick" if we want. For example, when selling broadband, customers often ask something like, "But is it sure the internet will work all the time, without interruption?" There are a lot of salespeople who say they will, and when there is a problem, some unforeseen peculiarity that makes the network oscillate, this buyer will call us screaming, claiming that at the time of sale he was informed that the internet would never fail. It is at these times that we lose the customer to the competition. It is impossible for any provider to guarantee 100% network uptime all the time, but I can guarantee that the rate is 99%. At these times I say, "It's very rare to happen, but if it happens, I assure you that you can call me, and I'll be there to help you." Even at the risk of losing the sale, I am always honest and advise the team to do the same. With this stance, we sell increasingly and get customers who become our fans. We do not want to make just one sale; we want a loyal customer, and we seek longevity in contracts to achieve our goals as well as our personal dreams.

This attitude of mine is also a way of trying to "fix" the bad name that many bad sellers leave in the market. Because of misconceptions on the part of some, the salesperson is often referred to as "unreliable". I prioritize being transparent above all because I know how important it is to achieve business success and my personal sales goals. I prioritize transparency first, just to end this idea that the seller promises and does not deliver. It is an important attitude to end this stigma and convey credibility.

The good seller cannot under any circumstances deceive the customer. He must work clearly, give details of the product or service, be didactic and honest in every proposal. If the customer asks for something they cannot offer or adapt because your product or service does not meet that need, tell the truth. Show the good points of what you have, but be honest about what you do not have, by saying something like, "What I have best for what you need right now is this option X [explaining what you have], but what you asked me I do not have it.

In situations like this we clearly understand the importance of prior research and preparation, because sometimes you do not have what the buyer asked for, but you know that no one else does. You can talk about this during the visit, as follows: "I don't have what you asked me, I'm being transparent with you, but I say it will be difficult for you to find this, because I know the market well and I know that no competitor has it."

It is the kind of approach that can only be done if you are well prepared, know your market and the competition thoroughly, and that will make all the difference in the buyer's decision making.

Also, do not mention that you will be able to adapt the proposal if this is not possible. Do not promise that your product or service will allow something if it is not true. If you are not transparent in every trade, when you close the deal, everything will go downhill. Or worse, you may close, but have serious problems when the customer realizes they have been defrauded. You will never sell to him or his network again. Your deceiver image will be marked forever. Remember: the seller carries your reputation wherever you are. In the future, you may represent another company, product, or service. Everyone you have dealt with in the past will be part of your career as a professional and will carry the memories of your performance, both positive and negative. The most common thing is for a salesperson to offer various products to the same customers when they change companies. Their credibility, therefore, cannot be compromised under any circumstances.

Adaptability

It often happens that we do everything right until the visit: plan, be transparent in conversations, and suddenly be surprised by a completely unforeseen and unexpected request from the customer. Suppose you have prepared to offer the most diverse pencil models, but the buyer asks for a model with an eraser on the top, which you did not imagine. It might even have been able to couple the eraser, but this possibility was not considered during planning. However, it is possible that this really is an unrealistic request. In such circumstances, it is important to be able to adapt, both instantaneously and through re-planning, depending on the complexity of what you have been asked to do.

Do not try to skip steps in the face of a thoughtless request, which would mean ignoring the sudden request and trying to push the customer's "throat down" what you already have, just to hit your goal quickly. It would say something like, "Look, close it that way, just one pencil will help you and you can buy the eraser separately later." Do not do it. Adapt to the new reality. This adaptive capacity would go something like this: "You asked me for something I was not really prepared to offer. I have nothing ready to show you now, but I can build a portfolio of it and bring you a competitive proposition."

As much as you have prepared to avoid unforeseen events and expedite sales, you must have the ability to know what to do if the unimaginable happens. Not everything goes the way we planned, because reinforcement, selling is not an exact science. Do not be frustrated and move on, as happens often.

Most of the time, you must go back to redesign the proposal. It is like I have said countless times, the more customized and consultative the sale, the more back and forth between the planning and execution steps will be needed. In these situations, take advantage of everything you have planned, give references to talk about what you have, explain how it works and what the product or service might look like with the extra you were asked for. Listen carefully to the request, absorb, have discipline, come back, and redo all the planning. Schedule the next visit to offer the new solution to the customer.

I have an example of a sale where I was able to adapt to the proposal quickly, even during the visit. I accompanied a salesperson to offer an IT solution to a company. At the end of the negotiations, the client produced a completely unforeseen argument: He had enjoyed our proposal very much, but if he closed with us, he would lose an old employee who had been working on his team for years and would be replaced by our team. I did not think twice and immediately said, "No problem with that, we can hire him to work with us on your project and it will stay with you." It worked, and the client closed with us. It is the kind of adaptation that can be done without having to reschedule, but it requires the seller to think fast and, most importantly, to have autonomy to make that decision (I will talk more about it in the closing step). I knew at the time that it was possible to hire the client's employee and offered the option at the same time. Situations like this are impossible to anticipate during planning and require the salesperson to be shrewd, alert, create solutions and adapt his proposal.

The need for adaptation is part of everyday sales. I had a consumer experience that illustrates a seller's adaptive behavior in an electronics store. It was a simpler retail sale than the custom ones, but the professional knew how to adapt very well to my situation. I had recently moved to a new house and needed to buy two televisions, the priority being a large living room appliance. I reached the store and explained to the salesperson that I wanted a 49-inch television. She tried to persuade me to buy one out of 55, detailing all the benefits of the product, but I claimed that the model price was higher than I could afford because I would still spend on a second television which I wanted to install in another room. As soon as she knew that I could buy a second device, the salesperson immediately presented me with a promotion from the store: if I took the 55-inch model, I could buy the 42-inch model for US$ 150 more — below the price of the second device, which cost US$ 250. That salesperson did no miracles, but she was attentive and knew how to quickly adapt to my need. I took both for the promotion and was pleased. A while later, I decided to change a third TV in the house, went back to that store and bought it from the same salesperson because I had enjoyed her service.

An eye on body language

Throughout the conversation, the customer emits body signals that help the seller realize whether he or she is satisfied with the negotiation. These signals can be either explicit, whether the person speaks clearly what they are thinking, or implied, such as body language, tone of voice, or manner of speaking. Sometimes the caller says a "yes" which means "no". Of course, this happens in any interaction between two or more people, but as the salesperson must be a relationship expert, keeping an eye on what seems like a detail can help you develop your sales better.

I broadened my horizons about this after attending that course at Singularity University in a body language dynamic. At the start of the course, a theater director interacted so that the class knew each other but with one detail: no one could speak or write. There were 54 people trying to get to know each other only by body language. Thus, I learned that among the participants, the only one who had a professional career like mine was a French engineer, project manager in a large company. The others were all entrepreneurs or people with alternative careers, outside the traditional posts of the business world. I discovered all this because, during the dynamic, the facilitator was "throwing" preferences, and people with things in common were getting together.

I learned there how much we put aside body perceptions in everyday sales, even though we are true communicators. We use speech and writing stimulus a lot, either electronically or in person, but do not develop other skills. In the middle of a negotiation, it is possible to understand, through the look, the face, the posture, and the gestures of the client, whether he is enjoying what we present. Sometimes the person comments nothing but "says a lot" with signs such as stepping back in the chair, twitching the spine, frowning, crossing the arms, etc. All of this demonstrates some discontent and can mean something like, "I am not liking what you are telling me "Or "what I need isn't quite that." On the other hand, if the caller shows enthusiasm in the look, lightness in posture, approaches you in the chair and smiles, you may be saying with the body: "I enjoyed it and I will close."

Before participating in that dynamic, I knew intuitively about it, but I had never actually paid attention to these "details" in customer visits. I have always observed much more of what people said and wrote, not what they let on. After that experience, however, I began to pay attention to the body language of the people I talk to and to understand how they receive the information I pass to them. I noticed that the more signals we can pick up, the more effective we are during the negotiation, bringing correct arguments to what the customer wants to hear.

I remember doing this on a visit by Algar Telecom to a large bank in Sao Paulo. I was already a director and was in conversation with the top executives of that financial institution, alongside the salesperson responsible for the account. Our aim was to increase participation among the bank's telecommunications service providers. We sat with the customers and, as we had planned, we began to present the advancements of our company. We evolved by proposing the expansion of services in areas where we were able to offer competitive advantages over the competition. At one point, looking at the customers' faces, I realized that one of them was really enjoying the idea. He was vibrating. I saw him relaxed, without tension, growing inside. He seemed happy with what he was hearing. Our proposal sounded like music in his ears. However, the next colleague, who had the power of decision, had no reaction, and seemed apprehensive. Aware of this, I interrupted the presentation and spoke to this decision maker: "Look, your colleague liked our proposal very much, I can see from his eyes. But you look a little annoyed. What is the reason?". After this opening, the executive confessed that, more than ten years ago, a company that was part of our group had left him in the lurch to provide a service. So, he suspected if we were as good as we were talking.

We managed to get around the situation, get into a deal and even sell some more to that bank. I consider that my sensitivity to the decision maker's body language at that time was relevant to the success of the business. I could not ask anything, finished, and just left. He would buy from our company, maybe not. But thanks to my question, he was able to vent and took a heavy weight off his shoulders. They are the intangible factors of the negotiations.

Customer's habits and culture

I have already spoken at the planning stage about the importance of adapting to each client's cultural differences. This caution obviously continues in execution. In fact, research on who the customer is should be done precisely so that the seller is prepared for the time to be facing to face with him. Reinforcement: It is important to know that there are different people, backgrounds, personalities, and cultures. And most of the time, it will only be during the visit that we get to know the characteristics of the people we will talk to. At this point, in addition to the signs, it is important to be aware of the habits and posture of the individual to whom you want to sell. Pay attention to these details to surprise your customers and empathize with them.

There are sales relationships where the buyer cares much more about your word than contracts, for example. These are business that used to be done as unwritten agreement, or the equivalent of saying, "If you say, I trust you."

This does not mean that no contract will be signed with this customer, but that, realizing that the customer cares a lot more about what you say, it is important to convey that security and trust to him. For this, it is essential to remember the importance of transparency, as discussed in previous pages. Just say what you can do, otherwise, in the face of any problem this client will come to you nervous and disappointed, saying something like, "You said you would do such a thing, I trusted you, and now you let me down."

Emotional control

Execution is the stage that most emotionally demands from the seller. To be successful, you need to be on the go all the time, attentive, paying attention to every detail of the deal, being helpful and available to the client. Having that disposition and resilience with every sale is not always easy, but the high-performance salesperson who seeks to surpass the goals of the company and its people needs that vitality, energy, and balance to achieve them. Nothing comes for free, but with a lot of dedication.

When we are in front of the customer, a million things cross our mind. In addition to the demands of the conversation itself, we think of the goal we must hit, the next visit we will make, the personal desire we seek to achieve, and so on. Whenever a customer shows disinterest, asks for reformulation of the proposal or something unforeseen, for example, we often become discouraged, anxious, or nervous, but these feelings only hurt our performance. Without emotional control, there is a risk of getting so tense during the sale that the customer will emit a series of signals and we will not notice them because we are concerned only with ourselves. So, you need to be calm, understand what the customer is talking about, breathe and follow in the negotiation.

It is important not to let yourself down, have discipline, control, and balance, face route changes and unforeseen events as part of the game, and understand the customer. Not letting him know that you have been shaken or upset by changes that have been requested by him will give you security. Never get dry, harsh, or let the potential buyer know that it has hurt you because you changed the offer, no matter how much you feel it happened. If you lack balance and get too caught up in the obstacles, you will not have the rationality to continue conducting the sale. This calm will allow you to act professionally, reschedule and return for a second visit, third, fourth, fifth, or as many as needed.

Another factor that increases salesperson anxiety and stress is that technology leaves us plugged in 24 hours nowadays. As we need to be available all the time, when we see we are already working all day - answering phone calls, answering messages on WhatsApp, or sending emails. This only makes the salesperson's routine even more unpredictable. There is no routine in the salesperson's life: every day we are in one place, eating different things and traveling frequently.

Therefore, I believe in the importance of working emotional balance. I also suggest taking time for health care, eating well, and getting a good night's sleep. Something that has always helped me with emotional control is physical exercise. They balance me and bring the vitality I need in my profession, as well as driving away laziness when it threatens to hit. I run every day, and, on weekends, I always try to practice some sport. At these times, I forget the problems and compose myself. I do it because I like it, but it helps me a lot to relieve the stress and tension of some tough negotiations, or the pressure to hit a challenging goal. I believe that if I did not play sports, I would be a stressed person and not perform so well. I found a way to accomplish this through exercise, but each can discover their own escape valve. I know coworkers who do meditation and theater, among other hobbies.

Creativity and innovation

It is mandatory that every salesperson has ready, from the planning stage, a portfolio of what he can offer the customer at the time of execution. However, to do beyond average, the timing of execution requires you to be alert not only to adapt but also to create and innovate.

As creative and innovative as you are when planning, there are insights and ideas that only come up during the visit. Of course, it is necessary to create and think creatively throughout the sales process, but in execution it is important to realize the customer's tips so as not to waste any opportunity. As the popular saying goes, "saddled horse does not pass twice". The saddled horse may pass only once in your life, and that is when you must ride it.

Openness to creativity is closely related to two points that I discussed earlier: adaptability and reading body language. The customer gives many tips, so stay tuned between the lines. Pay attention to what really can "touch his heart".

An experience I have lived exemplifies well what I mean by being creative and innovative in execution. I was still working as an Algar Telecom salesperson in Campinas, Brazil, and we identified a potential client that had a factory in the city. I went to the visit to sell well prepared, had a great presentation, convincingly showed our product and service. But I realized that even though he listened to me and showed some interest, he hinted that he would compare me to the competition and still not close the deal. A while later, he asked if I was from the city. I replied that I was born in Itajubá, in Minas Gerais state, Brazil. Behold, he revealed to me that he was setting up a factory in Minas Gerais, Poços de Caldas city, but was facing a problem with a telecommunications provider there. Immediately, I remembered that the services of my company were coming to Poços de Caldas and made sure that I could serve him. This information completely changed the course of the negotiation. He immediately said: "If you meet me in Poços de Caldas, I will close the deal because there is no player who has offered me so far." From there, the conversations flowed well, and we closed. It is the kind of situation that required me to have prior knowledge of the company I work for, something that is essential and must be done at the planning stage, but that also requires creativity, insight, and adaptation during execution.

On another occasion, for example, a customer was afraid to buy from me because he did not know me. I promptly told him: "Do the following, I sell it to you, I come here to install the equipment, and if you don't like it, I'll take it off." It was the kind of situation that if I let it go, the competitor could come in the next day and close a deal, and I would lose the sale.

Create execution needs

Customer tips and signals can also help you see opportunities and create needs that were not anticipated at the planning stage. This light can come from unthinkable things, so it is important to be aware of everything the person says and demonstrates during the conversation, even if it is spontaneous or informal. From something momentary, you can create a new need beyond what you had planned and close the sale.

I once went to sell telecommunication services to an open TV group. I got there with the basic proposal, which I defended very well. But the customer gave signs that he would not buy because he had been well-served for a long time at competitive prices by traditional competitors. During the meeting, we were walking in an open space near the television studios, and I was struck by a giant antenna there. Although I was a telecommunications engineer, I had never seen a tower as tall as this, and I commented informally on my impressions, curious to understand how the antenna worked. The client explained that it was sending a signal to a hill that, in turn, transmitted it to the rest of the city. Then he added that he had a big problem, because the transmission equipment was old and eventually the antenna needed to be replaced to avoid the risk of accidents. As soon as I heard this last information, I had a big insight: I remembered that my company had an optic fiber connecting those two hills and, even without being properly prepared, said it had a solution to solve his problem, because we could rent our optic fiber for his company to transmit the signal underground and never worry about changing the antenna.

Negotiations advanced rapidly. The customer forgot about the telecom service I was selling and said he wanted the new solution I offered. It is an example of creating a need that the customer does not even know exists. I prepared the proposal, and we closed the deal. In the end, I sold something completely different from the original intention. The salesperson therefore must always be prepared to meet these needs and see new opportunities.

Sale on first visit

Although rare for complex sales, of course there are cases when a product or service is sold at the first meeting. The speed of the process varies by situation. As unusual as it is in custom sales, selling right away is a unique feature of your product, service, or target audience. If this is your reality, make it clear that your goal on the first visit is to show formatted solutions from your portfolio and sell. Often experience will show you the best way to do this.

I learned a strategy when, in 2013, I received from Algar Telecom the challenge of staying ahead of the SMB (small and medium sized business) division to increase our performance in this area. Until then, I had only sold to large companies - except for the only experience I had with SMB when I was a teenager and sold electronics components at my uncle's store in Itajubá, Brazil. I assumed the position believing that the sales strategy would be like that used with the large companies, but soon realized that I was sorely mistaken.

In selling to medium and small businesses, everything needs to be faster, because most of the time we are negotiating directly with the owner, there is no intermediation with the buyer or IT manager (the network manager, in the case of my area of expertise). The offer and sale of the product is made directly to this entrepreneur and must be fast because he does not want to discuss features or technical details, but rather have the problem solved (in my case, a fast and excellent quality internet). I had to reinvent myself. I thoroughly studied the world of medium and small businesses, took courses, visited establishments, went "see with my hand" and found, through trial and error, that with this target audience it was necessary to close already on the first visit. We had to prepare as much as possible to get to the establishment, on the scheduled day, already with a formatted solution, suitable for each area of operation, but without customization - because that is not what this kind of customer sought. If our seller presented the portfolio and left to come back another day with the proposal, in the meantime the competitor made the sale, because all the products were similar.

Note that the type of sales I just described has a short cycle and goes beyond the scope of personalization and consultative sales. Even so, the seller, in this case, also does a prior preparation work and, during the visit, listens and serves the customer in the best way possible, demonstrating all the product differentials, specially designed for that customer´s area, but in a short time. It needs to be fast because both the customer and the seller have no time to waste. The customer, as the owner of the business, accumulates many tasks and cannot spend much time talking with the seller. This, on the other hand, the seller has an extensive list of customers to visit and needs to be quick on the trigger because the less personalized the sale, the less time you have for each visit. There is one feature that this professional profile needs to have, which I call "Serial killer." That means getting to the point, paying attention to the right measure, and quickly arguing to close, "kill the sale," on the first visit.

Interpersonal Relationships in Sales

We can never forget that, despite being a professional relationship, the client is a human being who, like any other, has his good and bad days. As much as the person may have accepted you for a conversation, several external factors can influence this relationship. Always keep in mind that professional or personal problems arise at any time in our lives. Being aware of body language and other signals that the other sends out helps the exponential seller to understand if the caller is experiencing any difficulty at the time of the visit. Suppose the customer is yawning all the time during the conversation. It will be clear that he is sleepy, tired, may not have slept well the night before. This is not the best day to close a sale with this person. Realizing this is crucial when deciding to shorten the conversation and set up an upcoming meeting, to bring in new information and try to close on a day that the client is more willing to listen to you. Do not waste your time. This stance is related to the ability to adapt at the time of execution, as it is impossible to predict.

The salesperson's sympathy, attention and care are competitive differentials, never forget that. It is more common than we imagine a customer to close a sale because of the seller. We are human beings, and we like to be treated well. Often, the choice to buy occurs precisely because of how we are served by the salesperson - even more so when competitors' offers are similar.

Once, when I was a manager, I went with a salesperson to visit a customer. It was a simple sale, and we did the process normally as usual: we introduced the product, our differentials and listened to the buyer's demand. During the conversation, I decided to grab my tablet to write down what the customer was talking about, and unintentionally took a digital TV antenna out of my backpack. The customer saw the accessory and was very curious, asked for information about the operation of the device and wanted to know where I had bought it. From that moment on, I just could not get back to selling with him anymore and we left. After a few days, I was surprised by a call from the same client, with questions not about the proposal, but about the antenna. He asked if I could go to his company to help him buy one for himself, and we could talk about the proposal. I went, and it worked, but first I helped him buy the accessory, and only then did he say he liked the proposal and would close it with us. I have the feeling that being thoughtful about the antenna helped me make that sale. These are things that we cannot plan, so it is important to be always on, eyes open to intangibles. Maybe if I were not willing to help him with the antenna, he would not close the deal or, at the very least, take longer to decide on the purchase. These are immeasurable things that the salesperson must deal with wisely.

Our company sponsored Stock Car[13] events in Brazil, and on one occasion a customer commented that his son was crazy about that race. The purpose of the event was to invite clients and, knowing that he liked it, I invited him to go with his son. He was excited and happy and, in the end, bought it from us. Now, can we say he bought it just because we took him to see Stock Car? I do not know, but it helped. In sales,

---

[13] Automobile competition. Learn more at: www.stockcar.com.br Accessed March 14, 2019.

preparations aside, the human relationship side is important. So, I repeat: to sell, you must like people and to relate. You must be willing to chat a little before and after each meeting, talk about random subjects, amenities, and feel the rhythm of each client.

As I have said a few times, I have always enjoyed talking with and relating to the most diverse people. I have no doubt how much this helps me in business. But I do it because I really like it, nothing is forced, and I even be friends with many clients. I consider that each visit, rather than a sales relationship, is the relationship of the salesperson to the customer. The quality of this relationship goes on forever, and regardless of the company the seller works for in the future, he or she will always be remembered as an individual. In the end, if you always treat people well and maintain good relationships with them, it will be much easier to look for them again with other business offers in the future. Humanity is precisely the great differential of the seller. If you are going to be a boring salesperson and technician, the computer already exists and replaces that kind of selling very well.

Already personalized and consultative sales require this exchange, this contact. They need eye to eye, to understand the human being, human relationships, to be that person's consultant. The seller who does this will not be replaced by the technology. There is not enough space in the sales market for professionals who do not like to relate to people.

One of my hobbies is playing online poker, which I often do on weekends on the page of an overseas casino. However, there was a time when my life was busy, and I spent about two weeks without playing. That is when I was surprised by a call from a person speaking Portuguese, with a super personalized service. She said that she realized I was playing less and, as she was quite assiduous, offered me bonus chips for the next time. I know it was the computer that mapped my profile, but it felt good to realize that the company devoted it is time to getting someone who speaks my language to call me. Although I knew there were business interests behind that call, it was a personalized service that made me replay the site. Interestingly in this case is that the site had already offered me promotions other times electronically, which did not have the same effect on me as the phone call. Therefore, I argue that the human relationship is always a differential in selling. The more enjoyable the experience for the customer, the more likely they are to buy from you. Remember this at the time of your visit.

To recap the execution step

Throughout my career, I note that successful professionals are those who, in addition to knowing what they want, are committed to what they do, to selling, to the customer, and to the company they work for.

They give their word and deliver what they promise, are concerned about the results, and demonstrate this from the beginning of the negotiations.

They are transparent, clear and do not fool anyone just to close a deal.

They pay attention to customer signals during conversation, including body language.

They have emotional control to deal with unforeseen events, know the importance of their role as salespeople and demonstrate this at every stage of execution.

They do not do so simply because they are good, but because this is how a good reputation is built. Only then will the first sale become the second or third sale, and one customer may refer you to another.

Skilled salespeople like people and know that selling is a relationship between two or more people. Therefore, they are aware that building a trusting relationship is essential for a skilled professional.

Part 3 - Closing: From Natural Flow to "forced decision"

Many people think that closing a deal **is the hardest part of the sales process**, but I think that from the steps taken so far, the "closing", is the easiest. Given my professional background, I would say that, in more than half of the cases, closing a deal is just a consequence of very well-done previous phases.

Therefore, I constantly reinforce the need to prepare from the beginning. Executing the entire process with excellence and confidence, based on your dreams, makes all the difference. The big-thinking seller who is sure of what moves him at every step, who believes in the quality of what he sells, acts with inner truth, and gives the buyer confidence.

Think of me: You have reached the last step with a great reputation with the customer. He planned and prepared the visit very well, presented himself in the best way, identified the needs of the buyer and had a lot of patience in the relationship and in the adaptation of the proposal until reaching the best possible version. It has done everything right so far: it has earned his trust, presented what he wanted, listened to him, negotiated price, delivery, or service, and clarified all doubts. Having done this homework, the closure becomes spontaneous. In doing so, of course there will come a beautiful day when you will hear from the long-awaited customer: "I am pleased. We are going to close?".

In such cases, the above sentence comes when the customer realizes that you have already done exactly what they wanted. After that, the formalities, the last details of the contract are settled, and the sale is completed. However, it may be that before hitting the hammer the buyer produces a final surprise: he asks for a special payment condition or additional detail in the proposal - such as a 5% discount, increased payment term or the addition of an item for free. It is important that the salesperson be empowered to make last-minute decisions that create conditions for closing the deal. The ideal, at this stage, is to have the power to make concessions and accelerate sales. The seller must know how far to close. If the company you work for does not give you much freedom, fight over it by making clear the benefits that flexibility will bring you in closing - and preferably make the results appear. In the teams I managed, I always gave salespeople autonomy and made it clear how far they could get with discounts, concessions, and benefits. I have always encouraged them to make decisions by themselves. Without this power, it is more difficult for the salesperson to be exponential, as the process is time consuming, and he would have to interrupt the negotiation all the time to ask his boss for permission before giving the customer answers.

Autonomy, however, demands responsibility - and unfortunately not everyone is prepared for it. I have had irresponsible sellers who closed bids with conditions we could not offer, which is far from being an exponential attitude. However, when a person is safe, prepared, does different, innovative, well thought out things and brings satisfactory results. Closing requires this proactive and confident posture. Insecure salespeople are often unable to close a sale out of fear or because they do not have the autonomy to make decisions. Once a salesperson of mine took the attitude of offering one free internet for the administration of a commercial condominium with 40 commercial lease sheds. His reasoning was that when a new company went to rent one of the warehouses, the manager would recommend our services, and, in the end, we would have an advantage over the competition within the condominium. That is, we would no longer make a sale with the probability of closing 40. The strategy worked and became a success story within Algar Telecom to be implemented elsewhere. I applaud the attitude of a salesperson like this.

Formalities to close

Closing usually occurs without much mishap when following its natural path. It is recommended to leave the visit with a formal commitment from the signed client. Some companies require that the contract be already signed, others an email with the confirmation of purchase, an "ok" via WhatsApp or even the buyer's own word - varies from case to case. Either way, this commitment ensures that the sale has been closed and you can celebrate now as you are closer to reaching your goal.

An important recommendation when it comes to making a commitment and signing a contract is to continue with the approach of transparency that you approached at the execution stage. Before signing, review everything that was promised and agreed upon in the previous steps. Clarify doubts objectively to avoid future problems. Rest assured that all points have been addressed transparently and that the person has a real sense of what they are buying. Consider if you are being honest, if you have covered all the points of the contract and if there is no detail that you missed.

It is common for the seller to get excited about closing the deal and ignore some important points that should be clear to the customer before deciding. Whoever does this is a bad, average, occasional or opportunistic professional. The exponential seller does not do this. He has a purpose, a dream to realize, and is transparent because he knows how much he must lose if he is not. The moment you make a commitment to the customer, it is your credibility that is at stake.

I repeat what I said on previous pages: To be exponential and to build your virtuous sales cycle, you must sell much more, many other things, and to countless people. Your credibility matters and having a good reputation does not come for free, not by chance.

It happened to me, not just once, but several times, that customers were so desperate to buy that they were already asking, "Where do I sign?" Sometimes they did so because there had been some change in the company's schedule, and the project called for urgency, or simply because they were anxious. And I always said: "First I want to explain everything that is included in the proposal to know if it is clear to you." I always made a point of closing with a clear conscience because I was extremely transparent and clearly showed what the customer was buying.

Do not take advantage of customer anxiety

Sometimes it happens that the customer wants to buy as soon as possible, but the project is not yet mature enough or even the best option for their problem. The good seller does not take advantage of this anxiety just to close a sale and hit goals. Rather, it surrounds itself, makes clear all its conditions and what is best to do in each case. I remember the time I went to visit a client, the IT manager of a software company, who was very sure of what he needed. "I want this product," he said. However, during the conversation, it was clear to me that I had something much better to help him, and at a lower price. I clarified to the buyer that the product he was asking me for would cost more and not perform as he needed, adding that he would build a specific solution to solve his problem. I came back in a week with a good proposal, ideal for the needs of that company. In analyzing it, the IT manager was surprised and asked if I was "crazy" for offering something at a lower price than what he had asked me. I explained that, rather than closing a deal, what was essential for me was to offer a solution that he was satisfied with and that, by chance, was cheaper. The important thing would be to solve his problem. The customer even doubted me, but I insisted, I asked him to be calm, I assured him that I would install the product and, if it did not work, he could cancel the purchase without charging penalties (I had this autonomy). We installed everything, and it worked out more than right: the IT manager was completely satisfied and grateful.

Later I offered my product to a well-known newspaper in Campinas, Brazil. The person I spoke to did not know our company and asked me for a referral from a customer who was satisfied with our services. Among the recommendations, I named the IT manager of the software company where the newspaper person called and told me what they heard. The IT manager gave the following statement: "Algar Telecom I do not know if it is well, but Augusto is good. If he told you, you could trust."

This is what I mean when I stress the importance of being an honest, and helpful seller. By doing so, you win not only customers but fans. I could have been opportunistic and sold something more expensive to that IT manager. However, that would not suit him correctly and he would be dissatisfied. I would make the first sale, but certainly not the next. Being transparent brings this credibility to the long-term professional relationship. I am not talking about being a saint and turning down sales. That is not it. It is selling by being clear and offering the best option to become reliable, a customer reference, and making more sales. This is the idea.

This stance holds true for any segment, even retail shelf product sales - those that may someday be completely replaced by recent technologies. I once went to a store in person to buy a printer, and the first thing the salesperson did was ask me what I needed the equipment for. I explained that my children were supposed to print schoolwork, and the salesperson made the following recommendation: "If I were you, I wouldn't buy the one you're looking at." He explained that I would spend a lot more on buying ink cartridges and pointed me to a smaller, cheaper, more economical option that had more affordable cartridge prices. I was pleased with his guidance and to this day, when I needed to buy something for my computer, I went back to the same store, because that service gave me confidence.

And when does the closing not happen?

I have just described the natural course of a successful closing. However, as much as you conduct the entire process perfectly well, it may happen that the expected end never comes. Still from my professional experience, this happens up to 40% of the time. Therefore, the seller cannot be accommodated at the closing stage.

You will find that you are heading towards an unwanted outcome as you notice that the flow of sales is dragging on. It is that phase where you have already made all the adaptations that the client has requested, redone proposals, scheduled new visits, but have not yet received his "yes". I compare this moment with what jurists call the baffle: the abuse of appeals and the insistence on irrelevant points to delay the process. In sales, this can happen for several reasons. I mention the most common: the customer may be literally wrapping it and, deep down, will not close with you; something may have changed in his demand during this period and he is postponing closing on purpose; he gave up on the purchase and didn't have courage to tell you because he knows you were very dedicated; He really is still not satisfied with the proposal, will need a better refinement and you will have to go back to the execution step.

Of course, these are just some hypotheses of what may be happening. Something common in all of them is that the customer does not close, but also does not say if he will do so soon, i.e., is on the fence. Whatever reality you are facing, one thing is for sure: you will have to find it out, in a process that I have kindly termed "forced decision."

I call this forced decision action because in the process you will really put pressure on the customer to give you a response. The exponential seller has no time to lose because he is after a dream, has a goal to fulfill, and does not want to stay in a creeping selling process. This is not at all advantageous because it consumes energy that could be used effectively in new and successful sales. When you realize that you have done everything you could for the customer, who is at his or her limit of comings and goings and still shows no signs of closing, it is time to act.

It is important to be clear that this step is not to force the customer to close, but to make him decide and inform him of the reason for this "postponement." Most of the time, the buyer does not delay in bad faith, but because it has some limitation. You will understand which impediment is giving you the opportunity to speak. There are three answers:

- The customer wants to close, but has some

  obstacle to do so immediately;

- The proposal is not exactly what it wants yet, and you should go back to the execution phase, or even planning;

- The customer will not close the deal and tell you why.

Whatever the reason for the winding, it is always productive to force a response to:

- Try to overcome the impediment and create conditions to enable the sale;

- Go back to planning and execution and make a new proposal to close;

- End the sale execution and leave the door open for future opportunities.

The key objective of the "forced decision" is to move forward in a selling process that is stalled and disrupting your goals. You must leave the closing meeting with a decision, that is the big point. Be it buying (yes), committing to going back in the future (no) or redoing the proposal (maybe).

How to force a decision?

The exponential seller thinks about the long term and the quality of customer relationships from the beginning to the end of the sales process. No matter how effectively you are being tangled up, you cannot treat the customer badly or be rude when you are challenging him to decide. Even because you still want to be close with him, now or in the future, you also seek loyalty and a good relationship in new contacts with that person. So, you must persist - always very respectfully - to get the answer you so need. Bring subtlety in arguments for the buyer to open and reveal what problem behind this postponement. Having sensitivity is critical now, because you need to be sensitive to find out what status the customer is within the three possibilities I mentioned earlier.

To do this, I recommend following the posture of being transparent. Suppose you are visiting when you believed you would finally close, but instead the client gives signals - again reading the body language - that he will not yet hit the hammer, or ask for irrelevant adjustments to the proposal, giving understand that it will not advance after that. It is a pattern that often happens, and it is up to you to identify when it is time to stop this cycle. Gently give the customer the chance to speak.

An example is to say something like: "Look, I made all the modifications you asked me and presented them in detail. I understand that the solution I presented solves your problem and brings you benefits. However, I realize that for you it may not be as urgent as you were at the beginning of the process. Want to say something about it?" That way, the customer will speak up and explain what is going on. He may say that he has no more budget and will need to stop the process; who simply gave up and will no longer buy, etc. Whatever it is, it will give you an answer. At least, it always happened to me, because I always treated clients with education, respect, and a lot of attention. It is important not to be afraid of facing this challenge because you have built a relationship of trust and transparency from the beginning. If the customer does not close, and it could happen, you need to know that.

Again, there are actions for each of the three possible responses:

1. **The customer wants to close, but has some obstacle to do this immediately:**

If you feel that the customer wants to close, but something prevents them, such as a lack of budget or other details that you can solve, do everything you can to get around the situation. If he says he is out of money, for example, you can offer a business condition to help him. This has happened to me. I realized that the client wanted to close, had liked our proposal, but was unsure.

Something blocked him. When I opened it, he revealed that he had a lot of interest, but had no budget for that year. I said something like, "Thanks for telling me what's going on, can I make a proposal to try to solve your problem?" He accepted, and I continued: "Let's do the following, if you have no budget for this year, I install the product now and you start paying only in January next year." It was about October, and I could offer that payment condition. The customer was pleased with the proposal, we signed the contract with the new form of payment and closed the sale. If I had not forced the decision, it could make me wait early next year to close. With my posture, I anticipated the sale and gained time leaving for other sales opportunities. This is the advantage of forcing the customer to decide. This is the advantage of forcing the customer to decide.

Sometimes the impediment may be just the person you are dealing with. There was a time when I went to close the deal and started to "squeeze" the client to force the decision. I realized when I questioned the buyer who was conducting the process with me would like to close, but his director was not sure to close. I never had had contact with this director, but in my research, I discovered that the man had participated in a fiber optic project together with the CEO of my company in the past. I got my CEO's contact and asked him to help me by calling the director in question. He did that, and I closed the deal fast. Note once again the importance of networking to complete a sale.

2. The proposal is still not exactly the way it wants it, and you should go back to the execution phase, or even planning phase:

It may be that despite all that you have done so far, there are still details that need to be explored for the proposal to look exactly as the client needs. In this case, you will find that the buyer has many questions about the order, showing indecision. At these times, it is important to know how to distinguish whether the issues refer only to technical details that do not change the essence of the project, or whether there are adjustments that imply for return to execution or planning. If these are minor details, of little relevance, you should try to close as soon as possible and suggest adjusting later, without cost to the customer. One suggestion is to say something like, "Look, these details you are asking for are minimal, let us close? Rest assured; I will fix it for you later." By doing so, you anticipate meetings and remove barriers for the client to close the deal.

However, if the requested changes are large, and you feel that he really wants to close, be patient, have discipline and redo the project to look exactly as expected. Thus, you open the possibility to return with a flawless proposal and then finally close it.

3. The client will not close the deal and tell him the reason

There are cases where the client really got disinterested in the project, changed his mind, and did not want to close anymore. As much as this is not the answer you would like to hear, it is again necessary to keep emotional control and know how to finish the process. Do this only if you have done everything you can, given your best and evidenced that the customer does not even show signs of closing. Insisting on a sale that will not happen is harmful because it takes up your valuable time that could be spent on other prospects. Remember: You must make $ 1 million in sales in a month. Time, in this case, is your enemy.

To find out what really keeps the customer from moving forward, you can come up and say something like, "I realize that you are uninterested in what I am offering. Could you confirm that? I would like you to be honest and open to me about what is really happening. I understand that things change, and if you gave up, I would like to know so I do not bother you anymore." Of course, this is my way of speaking. Ideally, find your polite way of having this straightforward conversation with the customer to leave an opening for you to talk to in the future. Some cases the client say he really doesn't want it anymore and will come back to me if he wants to and there are cases where, in fact the client, in the next future, come back and close, so it is important always to keep the doors open. Of course, there are cases where the person will never look for you again, but it is part of the game, and knowing how to deal with it is essential for the successful seller.

Do not close doors

Leaving the door open for the future is especially important when we talk about customer relationships, whether they have closed with you. The exponential seller is not shaken by a "no," quite the opposite: he / she follows the same course of action taken from the beginning of the selling process. Remains confident, open, and available for future conversations and opportunities. If you have reached the closing stage and been able to open the customer to receive it a few times, it is because you aroused something positive in it, and the buyer at least liked your business and was interested in what you offered. Otherwise, he would not have even accepted hearing it. Nothing was haphazard, but the result of their effort and preparation. This person already knows you and has a positive disposition to receive you in the future. Do not waste it.

When you hear no, salespeople often get discouraged, get angry at their customers, feel tangled up, and think something like, "I'll never be back in this company." But then you must go back, because that person already knows you and it will be easier to make a new visit in the future. You do not have to do all the planning and research work either, because you already know the customer.

The correct thing is to think that it did not work out the first time, but the next time it will work. As a salesperson, I have had several cases of companies I wanted to sell to and "got a no" first, then I knocked on the door again and heard a yes. This is part of the salesperson's life. Do not get carried away by the emotions and remember that this is a business relationship in which the main person interested in getting things right is yourself.

It is therefore important to have emotional control, flexibility, and always leave the door open. If possible, leave the last meeting with the suggestion of making an appointment in the future to introduce new services or conditions. Ask the customer something like, "Can I come back to you in six months?" Take advantage of the argument he gave you not to close and use it to your advantage. If he says he has no budget now, ask for a suitable time to get back in touch. If he claims to have given up on the project, check his calendar to look for it within a few months, when he may have already changed his mind.

At the beginning of my career at Algar Telecom, I wanted to sell to internet providers. They buy links from carriers to resell and, as they usually buy in bulk, it was an advantageous sale for me. I clearly remember that I visited an internet provider several times, and always heard a negative from him, saying that he would close with the competitor. But I didn´t give up and I said I will be back. I knew that the competition contracts lasted 12 months, so I used to go back after nine months, to allow time to negotiate and close on time. He once closed with me. That is, you can never give up. It also happens a lot for the customer to close with the competition, but after having a terrible experience, the client contacts you again. Selling is easier when you already have a relationship history. Want an easier visit than this? I suggest you have a control sheet with the names of all customers who have not been close to you, the reasons, and dates for contacting you again. Nowadays, with technology, it is even easier to do this, either through the phonebook or through an application. So, do not forget: There will always be goals and dreams to be realized, and the exponential seller thinks long term.

Some time ago, for example, I changed my wife's car, and the salesperson offered me auto insurance. I refused it because I would transfer insurance from the previous car to the new one, paying only the difference. Immediately, the salesperson asked, "But when will this insurance expire? Can I contact you within this time?" I gave her the date, and she really came to me to make a proposal.

Have sensitivity to give up

At this closing stage, I am talking about cases where the customer has agreed to receive you at all stages of the sales process. You can force the decision only when this relationship has already been created. And any minimally experienced salesperson knows that this is not always the case, that is, many will leave you without an answer, will not receive it, and it will not be possible to close the deal.

At any stage of the sales process, it may happen that the seller is unable to advance the steps because the customer has simply disappeared from the map and is not responding to him or her. It is common for sales professionals to visit, present the proposal and then never receive a return, for example. At these times, unfortunately, you must be sensitive and know the time to give up. You will not sell to everyone. This is precisely why, at the planning stage, we map opportunities by considering the conversion rate. You need to be sensitive to interrupt steps, so you do not waste time. You did your best, but the customer does not answer you anymore? Do not waste your time betting all your coins on just one opportunity. Make the most of your time, which is your greatest asset. Go to the next one. And always remember: By the end of the month, you will have to sell enough to realize your personal dream.

Whether or not you get a response on closing also depends a lot on the kind of audience you deal with. When we sell to professional buyers, for example, it will not be necessary to work out all this sensitivity in the closing phase. Except for rare exceptions, this professional already says immediately that he does not want to buy or that he will only be close with you in the future, because he is used to dealing with it daily, his profession is to buy all day. This attitude, however, may be rarer when selling to a technician or expert who is a user of the service or product, as he or she is not a specialist in business relationships.

Typically, in sales for midsize and large companies, there are two interlocutors: the primary stakeholder or end user, whom I call the technical buyer, and the purchasing area, which in most companies is solely responsible for formalizing the business. I would say the salesperson's main job is to convince the end user of the product or service, because the purchasing area is usually not decisive, just discusses prices and payment terms. The salesperson must worry about pleasing who will use what he or she sells and talking directly to that person - which I have already covered in the planning and execution phases. When these steps are well taken, it is unlikely that the purchasing area will have a decisive stance in the sales process - unless its only differential is price or payment condition.

Close securely

There are salespeople who naturally have a longer closing time or have difficulty closing a deal. It is the professional who comes and goes several times, goes through the planning and execution stages, and cannot put a stop to the process. This has a lot to do with insecurity. For this reason, I insist on the key that the seller needs to plan, study, be prepared and understand the market in which he operates. Such postures strengthen a good closure. Empowerment, security, objectivity, and decision making are key factors when closing a deal.

I have had cases where good salespeople were clearly in the closing stage but could not hit the hammer. Sometimes the customer is already prepared to complete the purchase, but the seller himself is so insecure that he conveys this sentiment to the buyer, returning him to the previous steps. It is necessary to be aware that when it comes to the time to finish, it is to close and end either naturally, according to the regular process or forcing the customer's decision. Go to the decisive meeting with one certainty in mind: "I'm going to close, and if I go back, it's because of the client, not because of me."

The weight of emotional factor

As I pointed out, the seller is a professional who starts the month in debt, chasing the loss, the goal to hit. Your goal may not be monthly, but quarterly, semi-annually, or annually. Regardless, by the time this deadline expires, as much as you have made 200% of the previous period's goal, you are already in debt again. Life is like that for salespeople. The good seller is not shaken by this debt, quite the opposite: he uses it as a stimulus, a challenge to be overcome.

I once accompanied a salesperson on a visit at the end of the month, and he needed that sale to meet the goal. We went to visit a client he had known for a long time, from his account, with whom he had affinity. When we sat down, the client said he liked the proposal, but wanted to know what our differential was compared to the competitor. At the ready, the salesperson explained that our solution was customized to his specific need. The buyer countered by saying that the competitors was the same, and said, "Why should I buy from you?" The seller claimed everything: competitive price, good payment terms, quality, service follow-up. The customer justified that the competitor offered the same. It was clear that the buyer was playing the deal and gave one last card: "Give me one more reason to buy from you." The seller, who had already used all his arguments, said: "Buy to help me. You have known me for a long time, and I need to reach my monthly goal. So, you buy from me to help me." The customer bought it from him.

Of course, each sale is unique, and in that case the salesperson and customer relationship were old. The salesperson was at his limit and needed to reach the target, but the emotional side in situations like this can weigh on the final decision. The products and services were the same as our competitors, but the customer bought them because of the seller, to help him. If he had not built a good relationship, he would not have opened to that final argument and consequently would not have made the sale or reached the monthly goal.

The premium closing

One thing is certain: Some professionals are more skilled at certain stages of the sales process than others. As with everything in life, we find it easier with certain things and more difficult with others. There are salespeople who are exceptional at planning and executing but lock and perform poorly at closing. On the other hand, there are those who do not plan or perform very well but have great skill in closing the negotiation. Regardless of your profile, the important thing is to identify your weaknesses to improve them, always looking for better results.

Throughout my sales career, I have had the opportunity to work directly with a variety of people's profiles and have always tried to incorporate what I saw good in them. I realized that individuals with very technical characteristics, for example, have much difficulty closing a deal. This is not a rule, I do not want to generalize at all, but usually this is a more detailed profile that keeps developing the solution and likes to discuss specifics in the last step. The seller must do all of this, but must know the time to say no, put limits on the deal and close.

In my team, there was a spectacular salesperson in the closing phase called Luiz Gustavo Palestino - who today is a manager in our company. I venture to say that he is the greatest closing specialist I have ever met in my entire career. When I hired him, I realized that he was performing much better than the other salespeople on the team. When researching, his networking was particularly good, as he knew influential people to shorten the path to the final decision maker. Most notable, however, was how short the Palestino´s sales cycle was. He planned, visited the client for the first time, returned to draft the proposal, made the second visit, and was closing by the third. This speed is rare in consultative sales, as I explained earlier. I started to accompany him on his visits and noticed that once he felt secure that the proposal was good for the client, he immediately forced the client to decide. He was an objective salesperson, was not afraid, and knew how to put an end to the negotiation. At the time of signing the contract, the buyer read and asked: "But what about this detail here?" As whom wants another advantage over some point. Palestino had no doubts and, in a relaxed but safe tone, said: "Look, I did everything you wanted, now take this pen and sign this sh _ _!" The client was quiet and sighed. I was watching everything, and I was amazed. Obviously, my salesperson had enough intimacy with the buyer to make that comment. Each has their own sense of humor and strategy, and there are customers who are not open to comments like that. The most important thing in this story is to understand that the salesperson must know how and when to set limits, say no, and complete a deal.

I sometimes asked Palestino to accompany a colleague who had difficulty closing a deal. A specific salesperson was particularly good at planning and execution, but nothing objective when it came to finalizing a deal. Due to some personal difficulties, this professional could not force his clients to decide, he was ashamed to pressure them. I then asked the Palestinian to go with him to have a lunch with a potential client. The seller had done everything right by then, and the buyer was pleased with the proposal, but for some reason was postponing it to close. On the way back, the Palestinian brought the signed contract and told me that, in fact, my colleague was waiting for a client initiative to put an end to the matter. Towards the end of lunch, when he noticed the passivity of this colleague, Palestino quickly took the initiative, gave a slight force, and informed the client that he had taken the proposal for him to sign. If that salesperson had gone alone, he would not have done anything.

When I was about 25, I learned a lot about negotiating with an experienced salesperson named Edson Riera, already quoted in previous pages as one of the professionals who have been true mentors in my career. Riera must have been about 20 years older than me. I was still working at the Portuguese company Cabelte when I met him. He was one of the directors of the company but had already been municipal secretary of Industry in Itajubá city, Brazil, region of Cabelte Brazil headquarters. Because of this experience in the public sector, he was someone we always looked for when we needed to sell to a government agency. The first time I approached him was to help me in a bid for a power company called CHESF.

Riera was a quintessential salesperson, and I clung to him for experience. I was a young salesperson, had the technical component, but certain knowledge is only acquired with the voice of wisdom. This approach I had with him at the time brought more business for both me and him. As he took advantage of my youthful momentum, I benefited from his knowledge. It was a particularly good partnership for the company that we worked for and for us.

As we worked together, I realized qualities in him that I did not have and needed to learn. Until then, I knew how to approach clients very well, understood their problem and offered a workable solution, but I did not know when to stop, to quit conversations. It was common for me to accept any buyer's request to close soon. Riera told me it could not be like this that I had to be patient, that it was important to negotiate more and test the customer limit to get the best price I could sell. He taught me a lot of things like that. For the tactic to work, again you need to be aware of the buyer's signals and understand how much of what we offer is necessary for them. The customer does not buy because he is nice or because you are nice, but because you are solving his problem, be it personal, professional or the company where he works. Therefore, it is important for the seller to test this limit and not underestimate himself.

Riera could bluff and deal with the buyer. He got out of the price war with certain attitudes. If the customer asked for an excessive discount that exceeded the negotiable limits, he came off the table and said something like this: "I will only sell to you when you can offer me a price that I can make that meets your needs. Otherwise, I will not sell because I will not deliver to you with the expected quality, and you will be dissatisfied with me."

He used metaphors, word games and jokes at the negotiation table. One fact that struck me a lot was a book with Latin expressions on his desk. Once, he let out one of those Latin wisdoms in the middle of a visit. The client, without understanding, asked what they meant. It was something like "Alea jacta est," which means "Luck is on..." This gave contours and breaths for him to conduct the negotiation, increasing our margin.

Sometimes Riera exaggerated when telling an episode. At one meeting, I was with him at one of those power companies that wanted to buy a large amount of cable. The client wanted to align the values, showing that what we sold was above his budget, and asked: "You are selling at $ 5 a meter, can you do for $ 4.8 for me?". We did a little joke, some calculations, and agreed. But the buyer reflected and, unsatisfied, asked for more advantages. We took a new joke and said, "Okay, fine!" In the third round, the caller asked us to insert some extra products in the proposal but to keep the price. At that moment Riera stood up and began to tear off his belt and unbutton his pants. "What are you doing?" The customers asked. Behold, he answered, "I am unzipping my pants because I realize that you are trying to screw me." Everyone laughed, the customer ended up buying, and we did not give in to what he wanted. Riera had a lot of that comic side, along with a good deal of security.

Therefore, I always say: you must know how to say no. Understand what the customer needs, go deep into their needs, solve it, and not just sell it for the price. However, in the end, you as a salesperson represent a company and you want to make the best possible sale to make your personal dream (Moonshot) come true. Riera could say no in a smart way, sometimes comical, sometimes intellectual. And one good seller's quality is precisely this: knowing how to deny when he reaches his limit and unlock the negotiation.

To recap the closing step

The big point of this step is to leave the meeting with a customer decision.

When the seller is strategic and plans well from the beginning of the sales process, the chances of the buyer closing naturally are high.

However, for several reasons, there is a possibility that this will not happen. Something may be preventing the decision maker from closing, or he has simply given up on the purchase and has no courage to say it to you. In these situations, it is up to the salesperson to force the decision, because he has a dream, a focus and a goal, no time to waste.

For this, I recommend using strategies and leaving the closing with one:

- *"Yes": the customer makes the purchase decision;*
- *"No": Customer explains why it will not close, and the seller undertakes to look for it in the future;*
- *"Maybe": you need to go back to planning and execution and redo the proposal.*

Part 4 - After Sales: The Customer is Your Biggest Asset

After Sales is a step often ignored by some sellers who believe the process ends when the customer closes the purchase. However, the exponential seller, who seeks exponential results, is not content to sell only once and wants to build customer loyalty knows that the sales relationship does not end at that time.

We can consider the after sales to be the icing on the cake. Once you have taken all the previous steps with excellence, won the customer, been transparent, efficient, aroused credibility and well-regarded in this business relationship, why are you going to throw it all away? The exponential seller does not lose everything. He does the full service, "beard, hair and mustache," as the popular phrase goes.

After sales exists precisely to maintain your good reputation with the buyer and to ensure the execution of everything you promised them during the visits. It serves to support the customer and not abandon him after the sale is closed. This is a step of tracking if what you have sold is being delivered. Make sure that the buyer has received everything he has contracted, that the delivery was as agreed, within the time limit and with quality service.

In most cases, after the sale the customer begins to interact with other areas of the company you represent, but the "child" is still yours. To think that tracking delivery is the responsibility of a specific area, that part is no longer within your purview, is an attitude that will certainly keep you from the customer, losing the relationship and rapprochement that was hard earned in the previous steps. Remember: You got the sale, made a commitment to that person or company. Do not throw it away.

Until then, the buyer has only dealt with you, which is for him the main contact with the company. Because of this proximity, this person often calls you directly to talk about a problem or need with the order, before registering a problem at the call center. This is common because it was you who first established ties with him. Imagine how frustrating it would be if, after the sale, that person who handled everything with you comes to you and hears something like, "Oh, it's not me anymore." Because there are salespeople who do this and then do not understand why they do not close new sales.

Your role as salesperson is to make sure everything goes as agreed, offering to support and bring the customer closer to the new areas of the company with whom he will come in contact.

Support provides security during the delivery step and assists with troubleshooting if needed.

Remember all the effort you have made to secure that sale and do not throw it away now that the customer has everything to be happy about. The commitment made to him must be respected. There are a few simple attitudes that make all the difference in after sales, so that the buyer feels that he has not been abandoned and that it is worth having closed a deal with you. This will surely make them maintain an elevated level of satisfaction with your services and make you the first to be remembered when they need to buy again or make a recommendation to someone.

Keep an open channel with the customer

When you were still negotiating, you certainly maintained an active communication channel with the buyer, both in person and remotely (virtually, by phone, email, or WhatsApp). It is interesting that a few days after the purchase is closed, you use this same channel to see if everything is going well. Make sure the delivery is going as planned if it is being handled well and if you can help it with anything.

Go further and arrange a face-to-face visit to get a return of his experience and accompany him. Such an attitude builds trust and creates countless future opportunities because the customer is usually not expecting this visit after delivery. If you do that, be sure that he will look for you the next time you need to buy something related to what you sell. Most likely, you will be first on the list, and the customer will not even consult the competition. In some cases, he may even consult your competition because companies are required to do so, but he will consider you, negotiate with you, and refer you to others. If you change job and sell other things, you will surely be served and listened to by this customer, because he will trust your word, regardless of what you sell.

The seller's life is always busy, but try, if possible, to make this face-to-face after-sales visit. If you really do not have time, you can email or make a call, but be sure to follow along at this stage as well.

When I was a salesperson, I enjoyed personally visiting buyers after delivery, when everything was working normally, just to ask if they were happy and if everything was going according to what I had promised. I did not sell anything on this visit, just listened to the customer's return to make sure everything I had proposed was delivered. With that, I surprised the person, who was even more satisfied with me and the company.

Be proactive

Part of the after sales work involves circumventing any problems that may occur in the process of product delivery or service delivery.

And the seller cannot escape the scene if they occur.

I have had such a case as a salesperson, where we concluded that we could not deliver what we had promised to the customer. No one made a mistake, it was really a project that we believed would work, but then we saw that in practice it did not work. Imagine if, at that time, you - the person who was there throughout the negotiation and made the promise - disappeared from the map and asked the customer to work it out with the call center? That would surely cause him a bad reputation.

It is even at these times that the salesperson should be even more present, offering alternatives, solutions, and ensuring that the error will be fixed. Take responsibility, come back to the customer, show them the options to solve the issue, and ask if they agree with any of them.

At Algar Telecom, for all customers who receive our contract, we have sent together an escalation list, a list of business cards of all people in the company that can be triggered if a problem is not solved. The list starts at the call center and goes up to the CEO of the company. We give the customer the freedom to look for who they want to solve the problem.

Every human being likes to be well-treated

Again, I reinforce the obvious: The seller can never forget that he is dealing with humans. All of us, without exception, like to be treated well. And what is the tendency of who is treated well? Be satisfied. Remember what I said before: to sell, you need to like people. You cannot do the after sales artificially. You need to be considerate and show concern because you really want the other person to be satisfied so you can sell more often.

The "conquered customer" is the salesperson's greatest asset. Cultivate it all your life. By doing so, however much you may sell another product in the future, you will be able to offer anything to the customers you have conquered and who trust your word. The second sale is also much easier when a good after sale is made. The more effective this aftermarket is, the more virtuous the sales cycle is.

We can never forget that all the steps we talk about in this book are for one purpose: to be an exponential seller to make a big dream come true. Each sales phase should be worked with excellence, as we have our moonshot to guide us. The exceptional, exponential seller does nothing automatically by accident. The great differentials of this type of professional are the preparation and the sensitivity with human relations. This is the salesperson profile the market will need forever, even as technology evolves: that sales professional who deals with complex, consultative, personalized sales. The significant difference we have in relation to machines is precisely our ability to adapt, sensitivity, body language reading, attention and make the customer feel unique. It is preparation and planning, coupled with human contact and face-to-face dedication, that make the sale.

Take my case as an example: In my entire life, I have always sold products with little differentiation between the competition. The broadband internet all the competitors have. What makes a difference to the customer then? The customers can talk with me right away when they have a problem. They know you will be heard and that you will not talk to a machine. More than a product or service, I sell attention, quality service and contact with the human being.

Every complex, consultative, personalized sale is made from person to person. The customer not only buys your product, but he also buys your trust. When we buy something, we also want to have a good shopping experience. This is what is at stake, this is the most valuable asset of the exponential salesperson, who is making a sale today thinking about the next, his infallible system, his virtuous sales cycle.

Of course, the customer not only buys because of the seller, but also because they have a need to be met. In some specific cases, you still buy because the brand of the company that the seller represents is good. Even so, the more prepared the salesperson is, the more sales he will make. If you represent a strong brand or company and think you do not have to work hard to sell, you are wrong. And imagine how much you could boost your earnings if you honed your skills.

Goals Never End

Being a salesperson is a constant exercise in motivation because there will always be a sale waiting to be made. When you hit a goal, the next month you have another waiting for you. So, you must always reinvent yourself. This motivation, I insist, comes from your dream, your ambition, your personal fulfillment, your moonshot. This is what always guides the seller in each of the sales steps. In the end, this is the significant difference of the professional who thinks big. Knowing where to go is essential to figuring out how. The motivated salesperson studies more, deepens, demonstrates confidence, and transmits security to the customer. The motivation for doing more and better comes from this: from the dream that is set early in the planning process. Our personal projects change all the time, so it is important that this motivation be reviewed with each new phase of your life. And always know why you are selling what you sell.

I can say with absolute certainty that motivated sellers are the ones who sell the most. This is evident throughout my over 30 years of career, where I have accompanied more than 500 professionals on my teams or as co-workers.

Of course, just being motivated is not enough, but once salespeople are at a good readiness level, I have no doubt that those with the most internal motivation will perform better. Always remember this and look for what motivates you on every visit every day. Of course, we are not machines, there are days when we are not well, and unforeseen things happen all the time. However, even in these tough times, remembering your personal goals, dreams, and ambitions can give you strength not to give up, wake up, and go out to sell.

Appendix 1: The seller and the crisis ...

At the end of March 2020, when I was finishing this book, the world was facing the COVID-19 pandemic. Several countries had decreed quarantine for their population, limiting the circulation and contact between people in cities and restricting some commercial activities. **A great economic and health crisis was happening in the world ...**

At several meetings and events in which I participated (virtually of course!) I, as a sales researcher, was widely questioned by salespeople and company executives about what would be the impacts of the COVID-19 crisis in the B2B (Business to business) sales world.

I researched in a deep way investigating the behavior of B2B sales in some countries in the world: China, United States, Portugal, and Brazil. I interviewed more than 40 professionals specialized in consultative sales in these countries and asked them about how much the COVID19 pandemic was influencing their sales performance.

Interestingly and unanimously, salespeople reported that they had increased their efficiency and results and pointed out that the main reasons for this performance improvement were:

- **A greater number of interactions** with **customers** is due to the substitution of face-to-face visits with virtual meetings.

- **A decrease in the average closing time** of the sale due to the virtualization of the relationship.

- **A greater focus** of these salespeople on the sale of products and services to business segments less affected by the crisis, such as the food industry, agribusiness, and technology.

The findings obtained in this survey, combined with several professional experiences that I lived during the quarantine of COVID-19, motivated me to write some behaviors and attitudes that exponential salespeople should consider during and after the crisis:

Planning phase:

- Stay informed, study the crisis from different perspectives (economy, health, politics, and others) and analyze the impact in relation to the product or service that you sell.

• Don't let the crisis limit your Moonshot! There are always opportunities. Make your planning and direct your efforts to sell products and services to areas and people less affected by the crisis.

• Recalculate how much you need to sell to achieve your goals. Set new goals. You may need to sell more during the crisis than in a regular situation.

• Research and find out who your target audience is and map out what the customers are looking for. Identify which businesses are affected by the crisis and how essential the product or service you sell is to your potential customer.

• Analyze and plan the alternatives and agendas to interact with the client (virtual meetings, phone calls, messages, etc.).

Execution phase:

• Be creative, use animations and videos to make your proposal clearer and objective for the client.

• Choose for virtual visits, especially with customers who are already part of your relationship network. In prospective clients, a face-to-face visit is likely to be necessary, but opt for virtual interactions in the next stages of the negotiation.

• Explore a lot of social networks, apps, and software to communicate with the customer (While I was authoring this book the most common ones were Zoom, Google Meetings, WebEx, LinkedIn).

• In times of crisis, changes in people's behavior are quite common. Be aware of your customer's emotions. Respect and understand the best time to interact.

Closing phase:

• Again, give preference for virtual meetings at the closing stage. If you have reached this stage, the client already knows you and the "face-to-face" meeting is no longer needed.

• Use digital tools to obtain the client's formalization and signature in contracts, proposals, etc. There is a wide availability of authorized software for this purpose (Some examples: Adobe Sign, DocuSign)

After Sales:

• Intensify contacts with your customers. In crisis time, the product or service you have sold may be essential to the survival of the client's business. Be proactive, be available and offer all the necessary support.

Keep in mind: Crises come and go; they always generate learnings and changes (This is not a cliché!). Certainly, many of the behaviors and attitudes mentioned in the previous pages will create a new way of doing business.

The exponential salesperson always adapts to the new moment, takes advantage of opportunities, and uses them as a stimulus in search of his Moonshot.

Appendix 2: The power of the seller

I have to myself that being a **salesperson is powerful**. If you take inspiration from the ideas in this book and incorporate the attitude of a successful salesperson into your everyday life, you will realize the power in your hands. Unfortunately, sales tools and strategies can be used for opportunism. This is not the way I suggest to those who want to make this profession a means to realize their dreams and achieve great goals.

The intent with this work is that you, the salesperson who has come to these last pages, can get the message of how valuable the profession you have chosen to call yours. You can serve others with a purpose, believing in what you sell, and offer solutions to solve real problems in their lives or the companies they work for. You are not asking for a favor by offering your product or service, but by solving something that someone needs that can make all the difference to that individual or company.

Be aware of this potential and use it for the benefit of the customer. Be transparent with who is buying from you, understand your real needs, understand your body language. Know that behind the buyer you are negotiating with a human being. Always study and update. Perfect yourself as a sales professional.

I genuinely believe that once you master these sales tools and delve into all the areas I have tried to cover in this book, you will also improve yourself as a human being in all your relationships. You will be able to see your relationship with others in a new light; as buzzword as it may be selling is the art of relating. May you know how to combine this wisdom with your constant preparation and enter the virtuous sales cycle, constantly planting and reaping impressive results, and being a true exponential salesperson.

Appendix 3: Leveraging Artificial Intelligence in B2B Sales Processes

Artificial Intelligence (AI) is steadily **transforming the landscape of B2B sales, ushering in an era where sales professionals can harness this powerful technology to enhance their strategies, generate more leads, and drive more sales.** Here's how AI can be a pivotal ally in optimizing B2B sales processes:

1. Enhanced Lead Scoring:

AI analyzes multiple data points to score leads more effectively, enabling sales professionals to prioritize their efforts on leads that are more likely to convert. This results in more efficient use of time and resources.

2. Predictive Analytics:

By analyzing historical data, AI can predict which prospects are more likely to convert into customers. Sales professionals can leverage these insights to tailor their approaches and engage prospects more effectively.

3. Personalization at Scale:

AI facilitates mass personalization by analyzing vast amounts of data and delivering insights on individual buyer behaviors and preferences. This allows sales professionals to tailor their messages and offers to meet the specific needs and desires of each prospect, improving conversion rates.

4. Enhanced Communication:

Natural Language Processing (NLP), a subset of AI, helps in understanding and generating human language, allowing sales professionals to communicate more effectively with prospects through automated yet personalized emails, messages, and other channels.

5. Improved Product Recommendations:

AI algorithms analyze customer behavior, previous purchases, and other factors to suggest products or services that are more likely to be of interest to prospects, facilitating upselling and cross-selling opportunities.

6. Sales Forecasting:

AI provides more accurate sales forecasts through the analysis of various data points and trends, allowing sales teams to optimize their strategies and allocation of resources.

7. Automated Administrative Tasks:

AI automates routine tasks such as scheduling, data entry, and follow-up emails, freeing up sales professionals to focus more on interacting with customers and closing deals.

8. Enhanced Customer Insights:

AI provides deeper insights into customer needs, behaviors, and preferences by analyzing data from various sources, enabling sales professionals to understand their prospects better and to position their products or services more effectively.

9. Dynamic Pricing Models:

AI analyzes market demand, competitor prices, and other external factors to automatically adjust pricing to maximize profits or market share.

10. Real-time Analytics:

AI provides real-time analytics that help sales professionals in making informed decisions quickly, adapting their strategies to the evolving needs of the market and their prospects.

Practical Implementation:

To leverage AI effectively in B2B sales, sales professionals can consider the following steps:

Integrate AI Tools:

Integrate AI-driven CRM systems, chatbots, and other tools into the sales process.

Utilize AI-powered communication tools for more personalized and effective interaction with prospects.

Invest in Training:

Invest in training and development to equip the sales team with the necessary skills to leverage AI tools and insights effectively.

Data Strategy:

Develop a comprehensive data strategy to collect, analyze, and leverage data effectively for generating insights and making informed decisions.

Continuous Learning:

Keep abreast of the latest developments in AI and continuously explore new ways to leverage AI for improving sales outcomes.
Customer-Centric Approach:

Use AI insights to understand customer needs better and to develop customer-centric solutions and offers.

By adopting a strategic approach to AI implementation and focusing on creating value for customers, B2B sales professionals can harness the full potential of AI to enhance their sales processes and drive better business outcomes. The symbiosis of intelligent technology and human intuition can redefine the sales paradigm, enabling businesses to thrive in the competitive B2B landscape.